norman schmidt

great paper jets

Sterling Publishing Co., Inc. New York
A Sterling/Tamos Book

A Sterling / Tamos Book
© 1999 Norman Schmidt

Sterling Publishing Co., Inc.
387 Park Avenue South, New York, NY 10016

Tamos Books Inc.
300 Wales Avenue, Winnipeg, MB, Canada R2M 2S9

10   9   8   7   6   5   4   3   2   1

Distributed in Canada by Sterling Publishing Co., Inc.
c/o Canadian Manda Group, 1 Atlantic Avenue, Suite 105
Toronto, Ontario, Canada M6K 3E7
Distributed in Great Britain and Europe by Chris Lloyd
463 Ashley Road, Parkstone, Poole, Dorset, BH14 OAX, England
Distributed in Australia by Capricorn Link (Australia) Pty Ltd.
P.O. Box 6651, Baulkham Hills,
Business Centre, NSW 2153, Australia

Design   Norman Schmidt
Photography   Jerry Grajewski

Printed in China

Tamos Books Inc. acknowledges the financial support of the Government of Canada through the
Book Publishing Industry Development Program (BPIDP) for our publishing activities.

ISBN 0-8069-5886-3

contents

introduction

general instructions

A good work area for model building consists of a large flat surface for spreading things out and plenty of light to see what you are doing.

Jet engines, first used in military planes, are found today in all manner of aircraft ranging from fighters and commercial transports to sport planes. Some of these "jets" blaze across the sky faster than sound, and fly to the very edge of space. Because of their speed, jets have revolutionized aviation. They have shrunk the world. Now with sophisticated navigational aids to fly high above the weather, jets allow airlines to maintain reliable global schedules to quickly, safely, and comfortably transport thousands of people and tons of freight around the world every day. Jets are a transportation marvel.

The paper planes in this book are modeled after some important jets that have been built. They show how the speed afforded by jet power influenced a new sleek airplane shape. The paper models are constructed out of ordinary index card paper. They are obviously not jet powered but fly as paper gliders.

THE PARTS

The planes in this book are constructed with three main parts made up of smaller cut-out pieces, arranged and built up in layers:

1 fuselage with vertical stabilizer,
2 wings, and
3 horizontal stabilizer.

NOTE model parts are not cut out of the book.

If you have not cut paper with a craft knife, begin by making some practice cuts. In pencil draw some squares, triangles, and circles of various sizes on index card stock and cut them out. For straight cuts use a steel edged ruler to guide the knife; make freehand cuts for curved lines. Always cut by drawing the knife towards you and away from the hand used to hold the paper. Continue to practice until you are comfortable with the tools.

Use a sharp craft knife (an X-acto knife with a #11 blade) on a suitable cutting surface (an Olfa cutting mat). Practice cutting precisely on the line. Always keep the blade sharp.

NOTE The proportions of the airplanes represented in this book have been slightly altered in the paper models to suit the paper medium, and they are not in scale to each other.

To camber the wings hold between thumb and forefinger of both hands, as shown. Working from the wing root to the wingtip, gently massage the paper to give the upper surface a convex curvature.

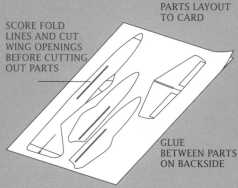

SCORE FOLD LINES AND CUT WING OPENINGS BEFORE CUTTING OUT PARTS

TACK-GLUE PARTS LAYOUT TO CARD

GLUE BETWEEN PARTS ON BACKSIDE

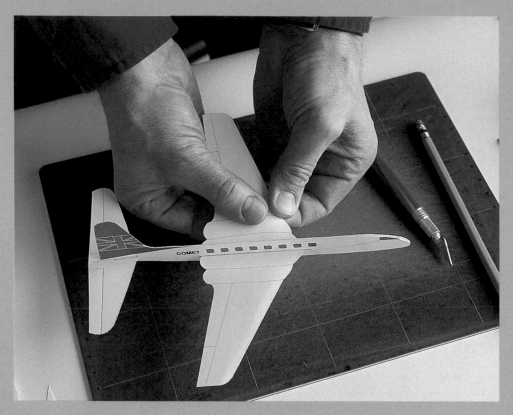

HOW TO PROCEED

FIRST make photocopies

Make *same-sized* photocopies (100%) of the pages containing the parts for building the paper airplanes.

SECOND prepare parts sheets

Cut the **parts layout section** from each photocopy, as indicated on the page, to fit a 5 x 8 inch standard index card. Then tack-glue to the card by applying glue to the areas *between* the parts (**on the backside**) aligning carefully with the edges of the card.

THIRD advanced planning

Before beginning to cut out the parts, score those parts that will need to be bent later, and cut opening slits in fuselage parts. Score and cut precisely on the lines.

FOURTH cut out the parts

Cut out each part shown. This must be done carefully, since the success or failure of every other step depends on accurately made parts.

Cut through both the tacked on guide paper and the card stock underneath. Remove the part and discard the guide paper. This leaves a clean unmarked airplane part, ready for assembly. *Keep track of the parts by lightly writing the part number in pencil on the backside of each part.*

NOTE **For all the cut-out pieces, the side that faces up for cutting will be outward or upward facing on the finished plane. This is important for aerodynamic and aesthetic reasons because of the burr on the edges due to cutting.**

FIFTH build the fuselage

Follow the sequence shown in the diagrams given for each model. Begin with the number one fuselage part, adding the other smaller parts on each side to complete the fuselage. *Align parts carefully.* Take care to position the bent over parts accurately because they are the fastening tabs for wings and horizontal stabilizer.

Stick glue (e.g. Uhu Color Stic), white craft glue, or wood-type model airplane glue can be used. However, it is easier to manage the drying time and reduce warpage with stick glue.

When building up the main parts in layers, apply glue to the entire *smaller* surface to be fastened to a larger one. Press parts firmly together. Continue until the entire main part is completed.

The author holding a paper Comet, the first jet airliner. Test flights, straight glides, and games such as flying through hoops and spot landings can be done satisfactorily indoors. High speed and long distance flights must be done in wide open spaces away from obstacles and traffic.

Lay the assembled fuselage flat between clean sheets of paper underneath a weight (some heavy books) until the glue is sufficiently set. This will take between 30 and 45 minutes for stick glue, and several hours for white glue.

SIXTH build the wings

Symmetry is essential for wings. Again, align parts carefully. Special care must be taken in those wings consisting of two halves. Temporarily align the halves using masking tape on the bottom side until the joining piece on the topside is glued in place.

The dihedral angle (upward slanting of wings from center to tips) must be adjusted while the parts are being assembled (before the glue is set). Use the angle guide given with each model for details. If stick glue is used, simply prop up the wings at the tips until the glue has set. If white glue (or model glue) is used, drying the wings is complicated. Some means must be devised to keep each wing from warping while maintaining the dihedral angle.

When the glue is dry add decoration and color to the fuselage and wings, if desired.

SEVENTH put it all together

Apply glue to the bent-over tabs that join the wings and horizontal stabilizer to the fuselage. Align the wings and stabilizers carefully. Press glued parts together. *Adjust placement carefully, viewing the plane from the top, the* *front, and the back.* **Symmetry and straightness in the completed plane are essential**.

EIGHTH camber the wings

This is a critical step. Cambering the wings gives them their ability to generate aerodynamic lift. Holding a wing at the root between thumb and forefinger of both hands, gently massage the paper to give the upper surface a slight convex curvature or camber. Work carefully from the wing root toward the tip and back again. Make sure the left and right wing have the same amount of camber. Avoid kinking the paper. See the instructions for each model for the proper amount of camber.

NINTH test fly

The paper glider must be well trimmed (adjusted) before it can perform satisfactorily. See pages 36 and 82.

TENTH fly for fun

Paper gliders perform best out-of-doors in a light breeze in wide-open spaces, away from obstructions and traffic.

Messerschmitt Me 262
first operational jet

1

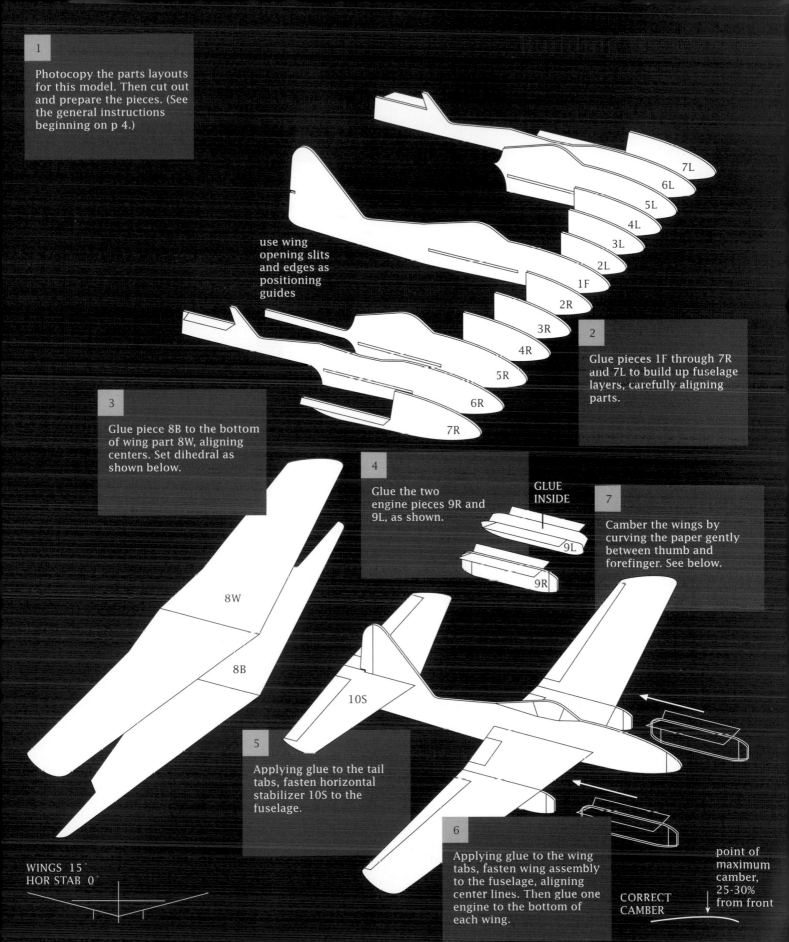

1

Photocopy the parts layouts for this model. Then cut out and prepare the pieces. (See the general instructions beginning on p 4.)

use wing opening slits and edges as positioning guides

7L
6L
5L
4L
3L
2L
1F
2R
3R
4R
5R
6R
7R

2

Glue pieces 1F through 7R and 7L to build up fuselage layers, carefully aligning parts.

3

Glue piece 8B to the bottom of wing part 8W, aligning centers. Set dihedral as shown below.

4

Glue the two engine pieces 9R and 9L, as shown.

GLUE INSIDE

9L

9R

7

Camber the wings by curving the paper gently between thumb and forefinger. See below.

8W

8B

10S

5

Applying glue to the tail tabs, fasten horizontal stabilizer 10S to the fuselage.

6

Applying glue to the wing tabs, fasten wing assembly to the fuselage, aligning center lines. Then glue one engine to the bottom of each wing.

WINGS 15°
HOR STAB 0°

CORRECT CAMBER

point of maximum camber, 25-30% from front

PARTS LAYOUT – Me 262

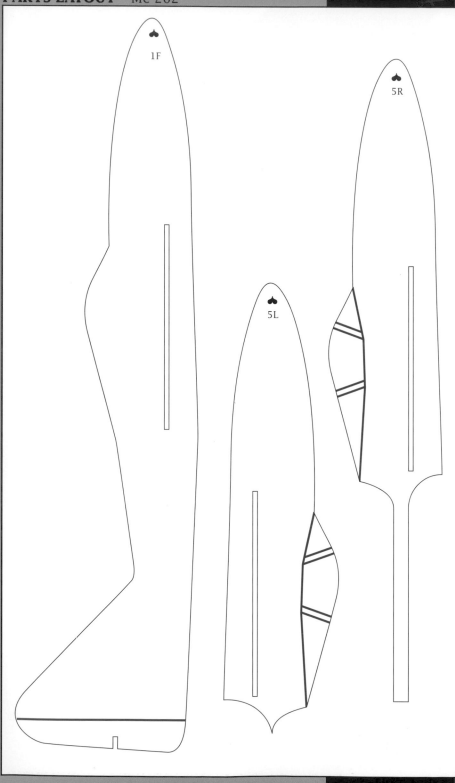

the story of jet propulsion

The need for speed first became evident during the Second World War as pilots pushed their planes to the limit, climbing, turning, and diving to maintain advantageous positions. Because the fastest fighters were most likely to be victorious in air combat, and the highest flying bombers were out of harm's way from ground defense, airplane designers tried to squeeze more and more power from the combination of piston engines and spinning propellers in the attempt to create faster and higher flying machines. The quest for speed eventually led to the invention of the jet-propelled airplane. Jets fly very fast.

Most people consider jet power to be an entirely new invention, yet its first demonstration took place more than 2000 years ago. It took all of the intervening years to discover how to put it to practical use.

Consider this background. In the year 100 B.C. an Egyptian inventor named Hero, built a steam jet. He noticed that water boiling vigorously in a kettle caused its lid to lift intermittently, letting out puffs of steam. He created a device to capture the power he saw in the steam. It consisted of a closed kettle fitted with a tube leading to a hollow sphere that was free to spin on the tube. On each side of the sphere were jet nozzles bent in opposite directions. When water

NOTE
- Cut on lines shown in black.
- Score lines in red.
- Use the blue lines as guides for adding details to the plane.
- ❥ Indicates the front edge of the piece.

was boiled in the kettle, steam rose through the tube into the sphere where it collected. As pressure in the sphere increased, jets of steam shot from the bent pipes creating a thrusting force, which caused the sphere to spin rapidly.

Over the years various individuals in different places realized, as did Hero, that heated gases generate thrust with enough power to create motion. For example, in 1500 the Italian inventor and artist Leonardo da Vinci, suggested that smoke rising in a fireplace chimney might be captured in some kind of engine. The power of the hot chimney gases could then be used to turn a spit for roasting meat in the fireplace.

Ancient Chinese writings from about the time of Hero describe how eggs could be made to fly by using fire. In *Science and Civilization in China* (Cambridge, 1965, p. 596), J. Needham quotes, "Take an egg and remove the contents from the shell, then ignite a little mugwort tinder (inside the hole) so as to cause a strong current of air. The egg will of itself rise in the air and fly away."

More recent Chinese history records how, in 1232, "arrows of flying fire" were used in war. They effectively frightened the enemy and set fire to their encampments. The arrows were in fact rockets, propelled by a jet of flame escaping from a nozzle in the tail. Soon traders brought these rockets from

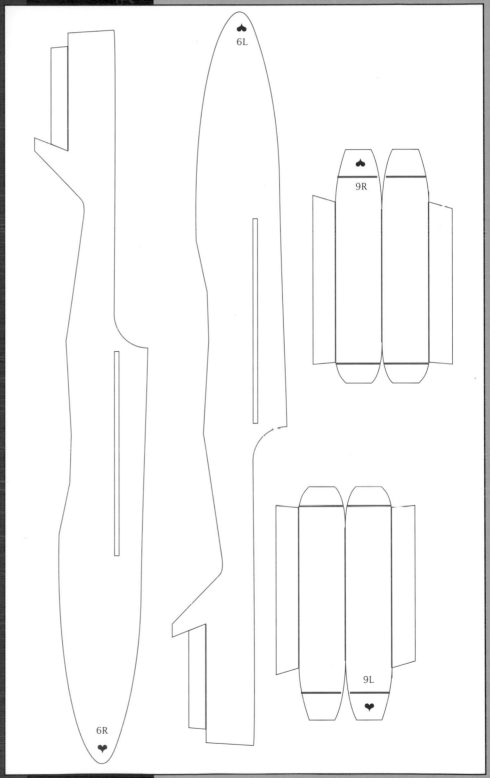

PARTS LAYOUT – Me 262

2R

3R

4R

7R

10S

7L

2L

3L

4L

China to Europe. Because of their simplicity jets of this type were built in large numbers before any other kinds. Besides their use in weaponry they were used as fireworks on festive occasions.

Another early example of jet propulsion is that of Ferdinand Verbiest, a Jesuit priest who lived in China in 1678 and built a model jet-propelled carriage. As did Hero's engine, it had a closed kettle and a tube leading to a collector. But instead of jets spinning a sphere, a nozzle came straight from the collector out the back end of the carriage. When water was boiled in the kettle, the thrust of the jet of hot steam escaping the nozzle drove the carriage forward.

FIGURE 1

Action and reaction

As a balloon is inflated, more and more air is squeezed in. The pressure inside is raised. As long as its opening is pinched shut, the pressure inside is equal in all directions. The balloon is stationary. When the opening is released, a jet of air rushes out with force in the direction of the opening. This action has an equal reaction in the opposite direction with enough force to propel the balloon across the room. This is jet propulsion.

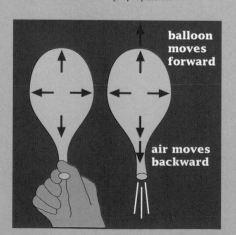

balloon moves forward

air moves backward

THE LAW OF NATURE AND JET PROPULSION

NOTE
• Cut on lines shown in black.
• Score lines in red.
• Use the blue lines as guides for adding details to the plane.
❯ Indicates the front edge of the piece.

NOTE
CUT OUT PHOTOCOPY ONLY

PARTS LAYOUT – Me 262

The inventors of long ago did not know how escaping gases generated power. Some believed, wrongly, that the streaming jet somehow pushed against the air to create a forward thrust. It wasn't until 1687 that the scientist Sir Isaac Newton described the principle correctly. This law of nature states that to every *action* there is an equal and opposite *reaction*.

Observe a frog jumping from a branch that is floating in a pond. The leaping *action* of the frog's legs sends it through the air in one direction. But the legs also apply a *reaction* against the floating branch, causing it to move in the opposite direction in the water – action, reaction.

Or take an ordinary balloon. As it is inflated by blowing into it, the air inside becomes pressurized as more and more air is squeezed in. As long as the opening is pinched shut nothing happens. But if you let go, the balloon shoots across the room. Why? As long as the opening is closed the pressure against the inside of the balloon is equal in all directions. But when it is opened a *jet of air* rushes out releasing pressure on that side of the balloon. The rushing jet is an *action* of the air in the direction of the opening. According to the law of nature there must be a *reaction* in the opposite direction inside the balloon with equal force – action, reaction. The balloon shoots across the room with the force of the reaction. The balloon is a simple jet engine.

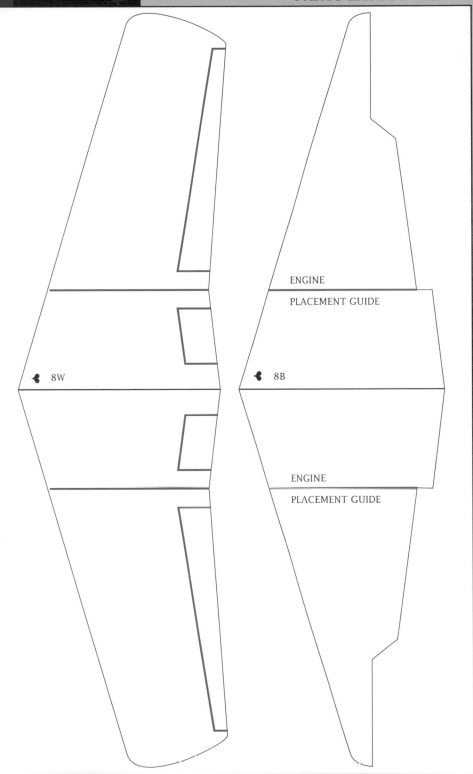

8W

8B

ENGINE

PLACEMENT GUIDE

ENGINE

PLACEMENT GUIDE

Gloster Meteor F1
speed record breaker

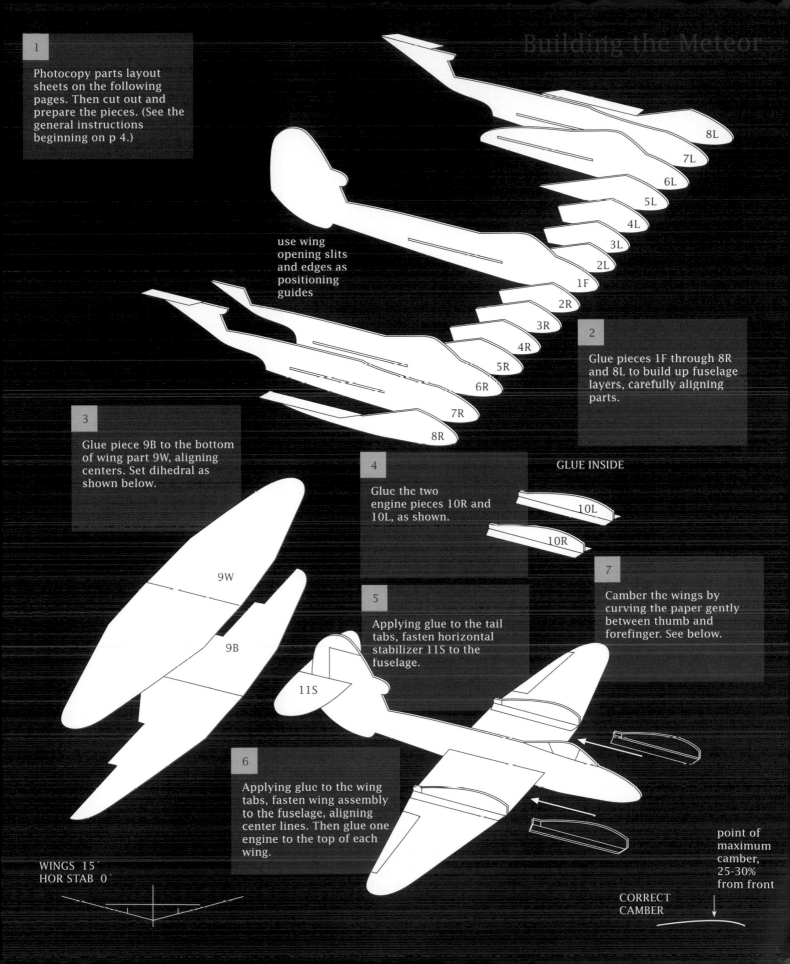

1
Photocopy parts layout sheets on the following pages. Then cut out and prepare the pieces. (See the general instructions beginning on p 4.)

use wing opening slits and edges as positioning guides

8L
7L
6L
5L
4L
3L
2L
1F
2R
3R
4R
5R
6R
7R
8R

2
Glue pieces 1F through 8R and 8L to build up fuselage layers, carefully aligning parts.

GLUE INSIDE

3
Glue piece 9B to the bottom of wing part 9W, aligning centers. Set dihedral as shown below.

4
Glue the two engine pieces 10R and 10L, as shown.

10L
10R

7
Camber the wings by curving the paper gently between thumb and forefinger. See below.

9W

9B

5
Applying glue to the tail tabs, fasten horizontal stabilizer 11S to the fuselage.

11S

6
Applying glue to the wing tabs, fasten wing assembly to the fuselage, aligning center lines. Then glue one engine to the top of each wing.

WINGS 15°
HOR STAB 0°

point of maximum camber, 25-30% from front

CORRECT CAMBER

PARTS LAYOUT – Meteor

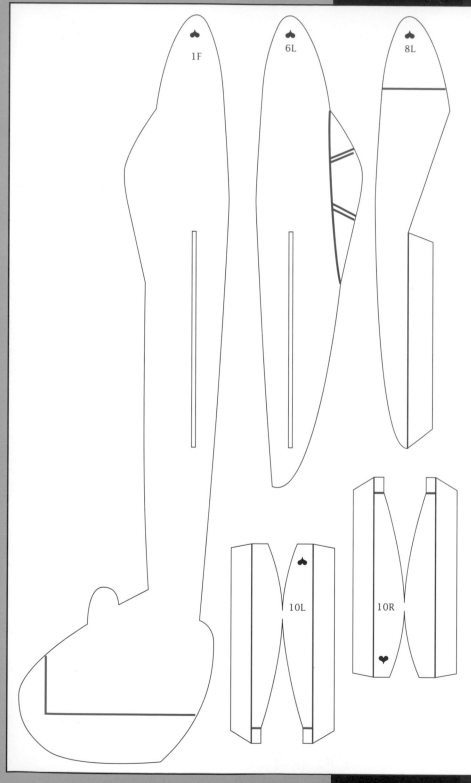

pioneers of modern jet airplanes

The success of a powered airplane depends on two basic components operating in unison. The first is the airframe, the structure and outer shape of a plane. The airframe determines how an airplane will behave when it moves through air, how it will handle, and how much it can carry. An airframe is designed to operate best within a particular speed and altitude range. The second component is the propulsion system, the means whereby the airframe is driven through the air. The combination of airframe and propulsion system determines how fast and how high an airplane can fly. If not enough power is supplied, the airframe cannot perform as well as possible. It might not get off the ground. If too much power is supplied, the airframe might handle poorly or break up in flight. The two components of airframe structure and propulsion system must be carefully matched for an airplane to be well balanced and controllable under various conditions.

In the time between the two world wars, air races were popular entertainment. Airplane designers everywhere tried to outdo each other in the attempt to win the prestigious races of the day. It was a matter of national pride. It was also important in the development of better airplanes.

The keen competition ultimately resulted in nimble racers that could exceed 400 miles per hour and could turn on a button. These planes had lightweight and strong airframes with efficient wings and were driven by giant piston engines swinging multi-bladed propellers. The giant engines used superchargers (air compressors) to pump additional air into the cylinders to boost power and were very heavy.

When the Second World War broke out, the competition for superior designs moved from the racecourse to the battlefield, and the technology that had been developed for racers was applied to fighters.

Wartime pilots pushed their planes to the limit. One thing noticed was that an overspeed dive introduced strange plane behavior. Sometimes control sticks became immovable or reversed their operation. Other times the airplanes simply went wildly out of control. Such unpredictable reactions were of major concern for airframe designers.

A NEW SOUND IN THE AIR

Always searching for airplane improvements, researchers in different places often come to similar conclusions about the same thing at the same time. Such was the case with jet propulsion. In the 1930s, a small workshop in Britain produced a loud sound not heard before. The same sound was heard in

NOTE
• Cut on lines shown in black.
• Score lines in red.
• Use the blue lines as guides for adding details to the plane.
❧ Indicates the front edge of the piece.

PARTS LAYOUT – Meteor

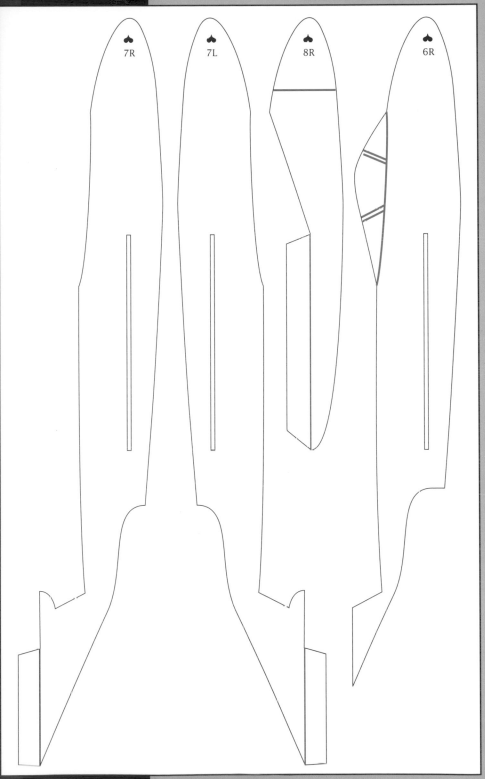

NOTE
- Cut on lines shown in black.
- Score lines in red.
- Use the blue lines as guides for adding details to the plane.
- ➤ Indicates the front edge of the piece.

PARTS LAYOUT – Meteor

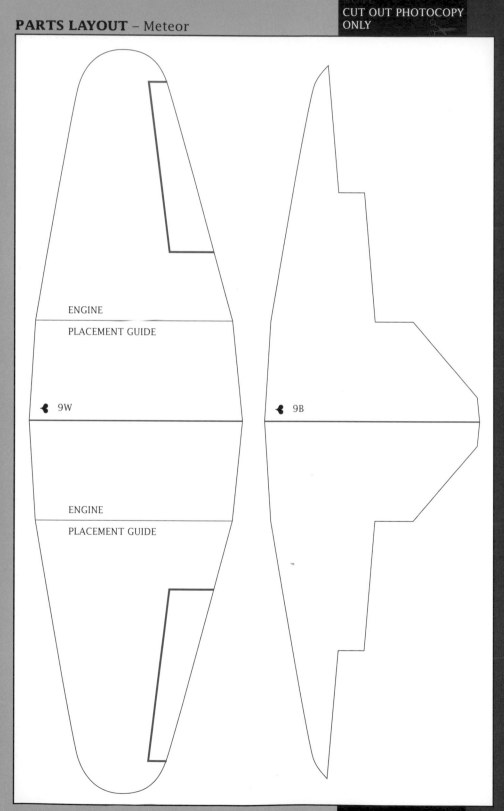

ENGINE

PLACEMENT GUIDE

➤ 9W

➤ 9B

ENGINE

PLACEMENT GUIDE

Germany. Two young engineers, Frank Whittle and Hans von Ohain, quite independently had realized that jet power, burning liquid fuel, might result in an engine with fewer moving parts. It would be lighter in weight than a piston engine, making it ideal for aircraft propulsion. On their own, and with little encouragement from big aircraft manufacturers or governments, these dedicated individuals carried out experiments with jet engines.

The basic operating principle of all jets that burn fuel internally is the same. They consist of a cylindrical tube in which fuel and an oxidizer are mixed and ignited. The resulting combustion greatly expands the volume of the gases, which shoot backwards out the exhaust pipe. The action of the jet of hot gases leaving the rear of the engine causes an equal reaction in a forward direction, which is the engine's thrust.

Both engineers realized that for such a jet to work satisfactorily in an airplane, and burn with enough vigor to produce thrust from a standing start, huge amounts of oxygen-rich air would be required in a steady supply. This meant that the air feeding the flame would have to be pressurized before being mixed with fuel. They both knew that this was possible only if the engine had an air compressor ahead of the flame. The compressor, in turn, could be driven by the thrust of combustion through a turbine located behind the flame and ahead of the exhaust pipe. This idea was not completely new, since these compressors were not unlike those found in the giant supercharged piston engines. This arrangement – compressor, combustion chamber, turbine, jet nozzle – was the magic formula for jet power that the engineers had simultaneously discovered. The new sound was the whine of the turbine and the roar of the jet flame. It was the turbojet. See p 76.

Few people, however, believed that these loud engines would ever amount to anything. The main problem was that jets run extremely hot and no materials existed that could withstand the heat for any length of time. The engines disintegrated after running only a short while.

As the war progressed, the demand for speed in the air increased. Speed meant superiority. Famous air battles, such as the Battle of Britain, had been won, in part, because of the superior speed and turning ability of fighter planes. Their agility came from perfectly matched airframes and propulsion systems. Although more speed was required, designers knew that no more speed or power could be squeezed from existing airframes or engines. The existing large supercharged piston engines were becoming too complicated to be practical, and propellers could not move

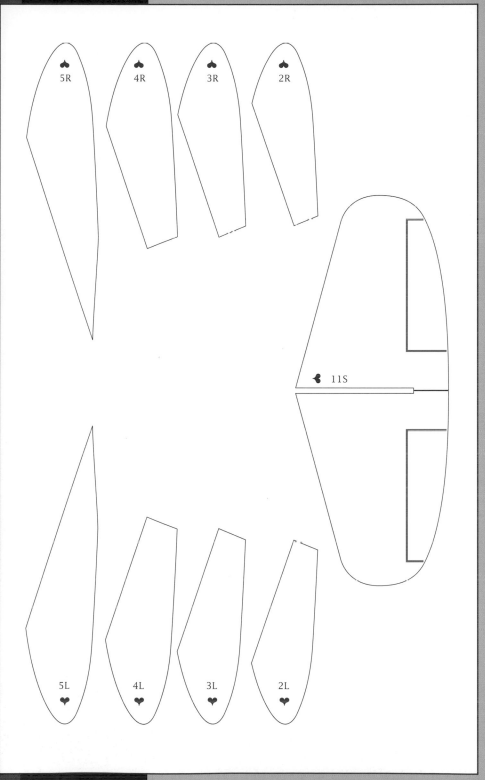

Lockheed P-80 Shooting Star
the long lived jet

1 Photocopy the parts layouts for this model. Then cut out and prepare the pieces. (See the general instructions beginning on p 4.)

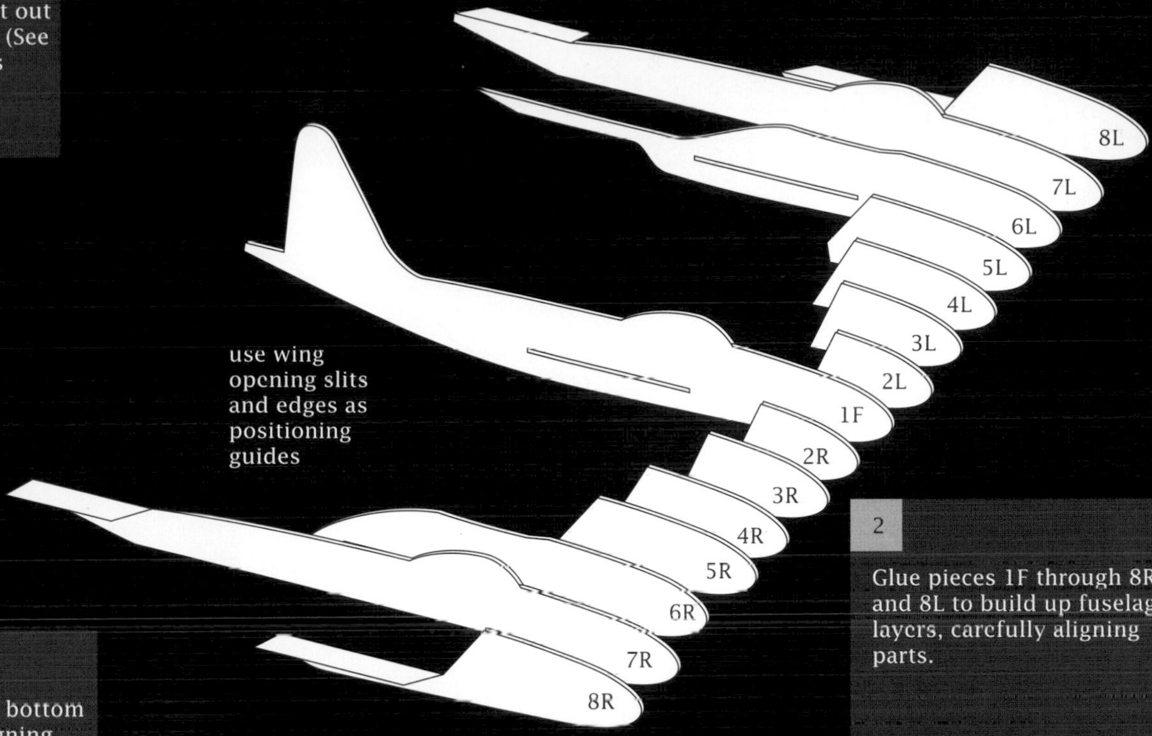

use wing opening slits and edges as positioning guides

8L
7L
6L
5L
4L
3L
2L
1F
2R
3R
4R
5R
6R
7R
8R

2 Glue pieces 1F through 8R and 8L to build up fuselage layers, carefully aligning parts.

3 Glue piece 9B to the bottom of wing part 9W, aligning centers. Set dihedral as shown below.

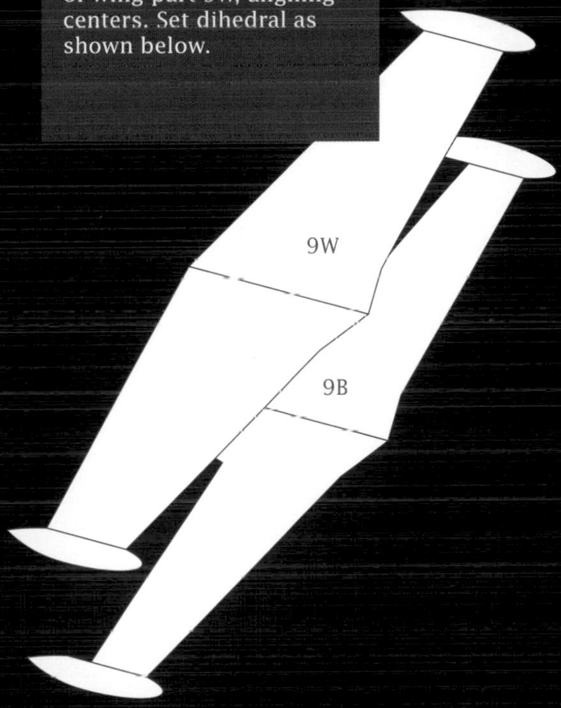

9W

9B

4 Applying glue to the tail tabs, fasten horizontal stabilizer 10S to the fuselage.

6 Camber the wings by curving the paper gently between thumb and forefinger. See below.

10S

5 Applying glue to the wing tabs, fasten wing assembly to the fuselage, aligning center lines. Then bend wing tip tanks down so that they are vertical.

WINGS 15°
HOR STAB 0°

point of maximum camber, 25-30% from front

CORRECT CAMBER

PARTS LAYOUT – P-80

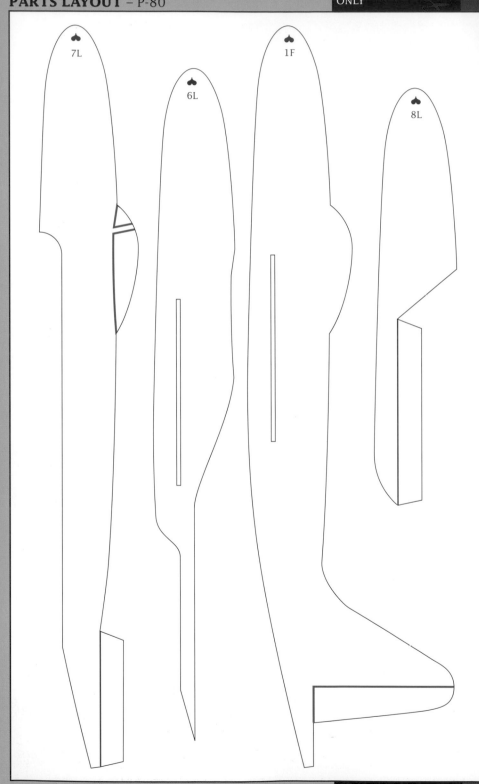

any more air, especially at high altitudes where there was less air to move. Besides, at very high speeds pilots could not control planes with the existing airframes. Wartime designers knew that an end had been reached in traditional aircraft technology and a new approach was needed. Whittle and von Ohain believed the answer to more power lay in jet propulsion. Airframe design was a separate problem that others needed to solve.

FIRST OPERATIONAL JETS

The first jet engines were cranky and unreliable. They burned huge amounts of fuel for their power, and had a service life measured only in minutes before they disintegrated. Jets could be of no use until heat tolerant metal alloys were developed. Because of the wartime demand for rapid advancement, these were forthcoming, and by using them, both engineers were able to run their jets for several hours at a time. Because of this both men convinced their governments to back jet research.

Thereafter development was rapid and jet propulsion systems of various kinds appeared. Research teams were established. In both Britain and Germany various experimental jet-powered planes were tested with increasing success.

By 1944 jet engines were reliable enough to move from the

NOTE
• Cut on lines shown in black.
• Score lines in red.
• Use the blue lines as guides for adding details to the plane.
❧ Indicates the front edge of the piece.

PARTS LAYOUT – P-80

laboratory to the battlefield. A Junkers turbojet engine was fitted to a Messerschmitt airframe. The plane was the Me 262. **(#1, p 6.)** Soon thereafter in Britain a Rolls-Royce turbojet was installed in a Gloster – the Meteor F1. **(#2, p 12.)** The results were spectacular. The planes were fast. The Me 262 flew a full 100 miles per hour faster than any piston powered plane. The Meteor was not far behind. Both turbojet fighters were built in quantity but never met in battle. The Me 262, the first operational jet, was considered the superior machine.

Rocket engines, too, were used. See p 73. Heinkel built the He 176 rocket-powered fighter, which saw limited service as a defense against Allied heavy bombers. The problem with rockets, the simplest jets, was that all their fuel burned up in only minutes. They were better suited to rocket-propelled weapons, which were in use on both sides by war's end. Rocket power was also used to boost a variety of planes into the air when heavily loaded. Once airborne their regular engines took over.

One jet research team, led by Paul Schmidt, conducted experiments with pulsejet engines. See p 75. The pulsejet was much simpler and lighter than the turbojet, but inefficient by comparison. However, it had a longer burn time than rocket engines, making it useful for a certain kind of aircraft. Towards the end of the war, when most

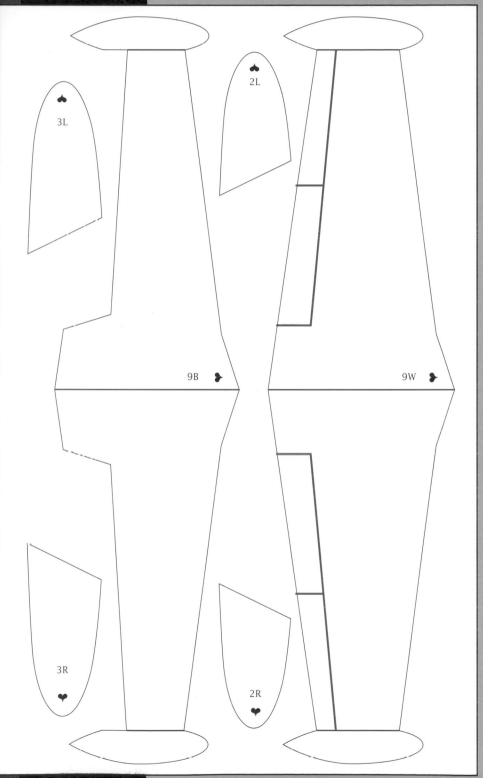

NOTE
- Cut on lines shown in black.
- Score lines in red.
- Use the blue lines as guides for adding details to the plane.
- ❥ Indicates the front edge of the piece.

PARTS LAYOUT – P-80

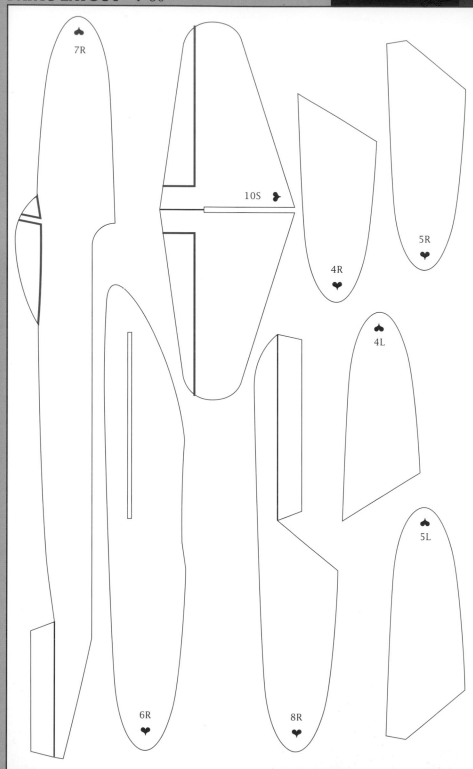

of the German airforce had been destroyed and they had few bombers and fewer pilots in the air, German engineers built a small airframe carrying a single bomb, powered with a pulsejet engine, known as the V-1 Buzzbomb. It had no pilot and was guided by a magnetic compass and clock mechanism. The pulsejet's loud stuttering roar terrified people even before the bomb exploded. Under circumstances of dwindling resources, it was a simple way of retaliating. It had just enough range to reach London from mainland Europe before running out of fuel. Many of these flying bombs were intercepted by the fast Meteor F1s, which marked the first jet-to-jet encounters.

By this time the war was nearly at an end. Of the various turbo-jet, pulsejet, and rocket-powered craft built by Germany, numbering more than one thousand, only a few ever saw service because there was little fuel to power them.

The demands of war had made jet power practical, even though it had come too late to influence air superiority. But its merits had been clearly demonstrated and the stage was set for this power to be applied widely. After the war, all German technology fell into the hands of the Allies, including their technology developed for jets, resulting in a rapid worldwide application of jet propulsion.

Mikoyan-Gurevich MiG-9
first Russian Jet

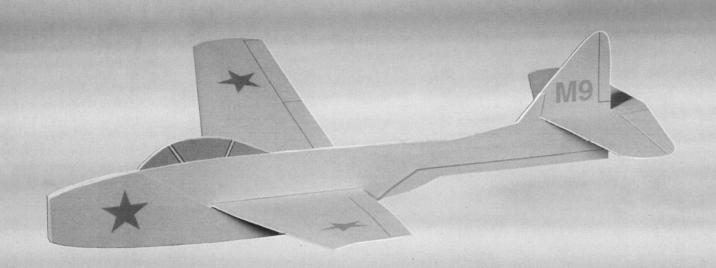

1

Photocopy the parts layouts for this model. Then cut out and prepare the pieces. (See the general instructions beginning on p 4.)

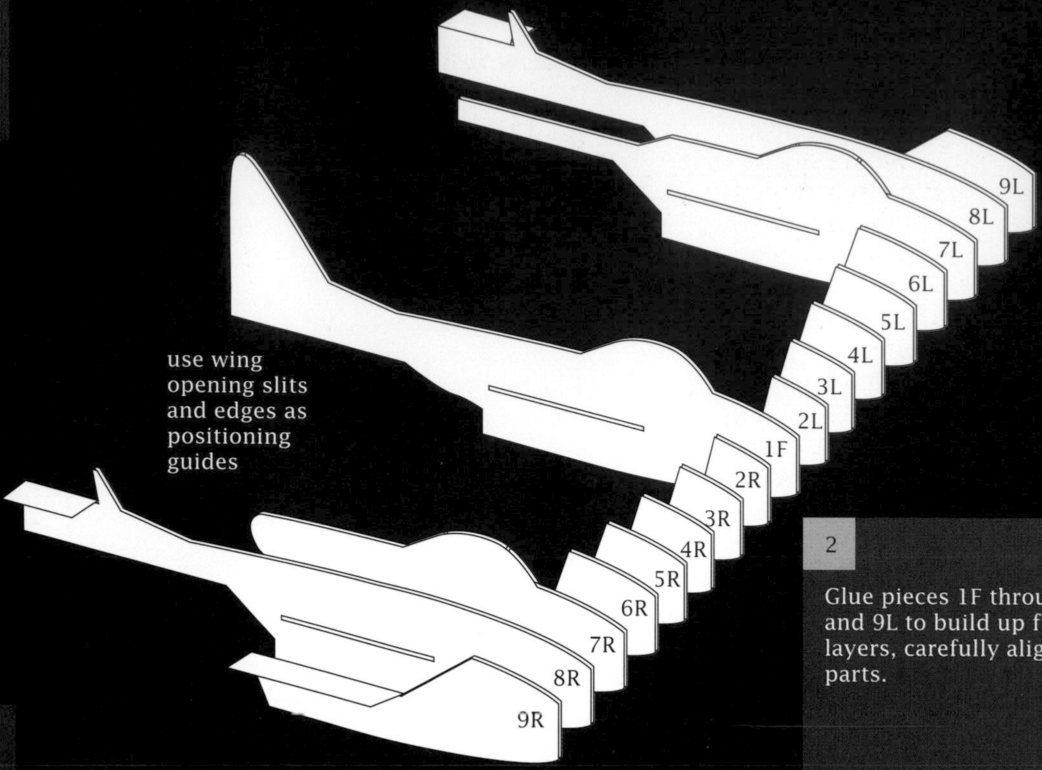

use wing opening slits and edges as positioning guides

9L
8L
7L
6L
5L
4L
3L
2L
1F
2R
3R
4R
5R
6R
7R
8R
9R

2

Glue pieces 1F through 9R and 9L to build up fuselage layers, carefully aligning parts.

3

Glue piece 10B to the bottom of wing part 10W, aligning centers. Set dihedral as shown below.

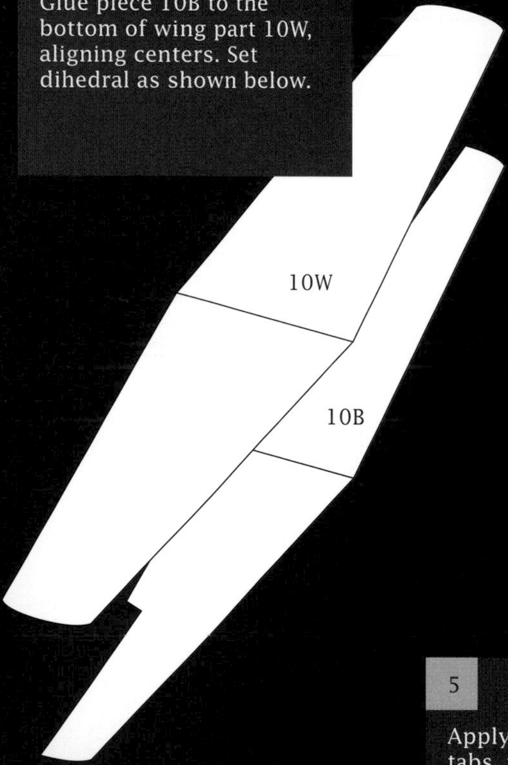

4

Applying glue to the tail tabs, fasten horizontal stabilizer 11S to the fuselage.

6

Camber the wings by curving the paper gently between thumb and forefinger. See below.

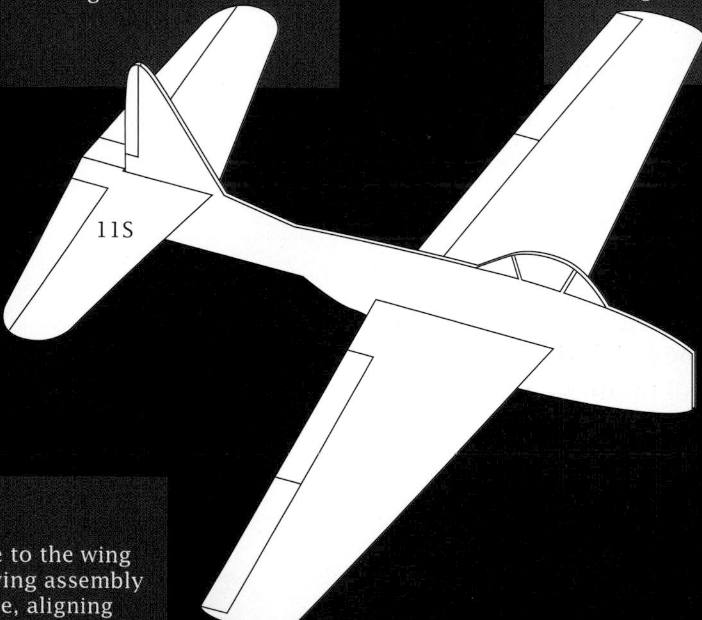

10W

10B

11S

5

Applying glue to the wing tabs, fasten wing assembly to the fuselage, aligning center lines.

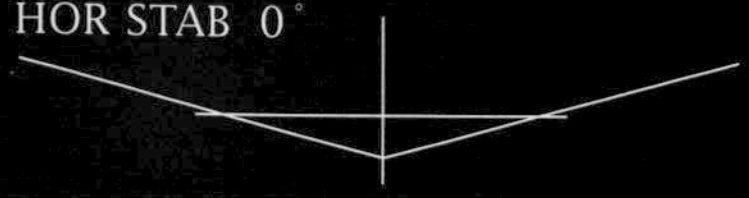

WINGS 15°
HOR STAB 0°

point of maximum camber, 25-30% from front

CORRECT CAMBER

the shape for high speed

All flight involves the creation of two forces by artificial means to oppose two forces occuring naturally — the force of *lift* must be created to counteract the earth's *gravity*, and the force of *thrust* to oppose air *resistance*. The new jets had plenty of power to overcome air resistance, with early models already matching the most powerful piston engines. The problem was that at very high speed air began to behave differently when flowing around solid objects than it did at low speed, and no one knew exactly what was happening. It was soon discovered how much the shape of an airframe determines airflow. The high speed of jets called for new and different shapes in airplanes.

SHAPE AND FLIGHT

To work, aircraft wings must alter air pressure. They do this in two ways.

First, as they move forward wings slice the surrounding air into two layers, one above and one beneath the wings. Both layers are made up of the same number of molecules. If the wing has a curved upper surface, the molecules moving across the top surface have farther to travel than the ones underneath. As they try to maintain their position in relation to the rest of the air molecules, they become spaced farther apart and their speed increases so that when they reach the back edge of the wing,

NOTE
- Cut on lines shown in black.
- Score lines in red.
- Use the blue lines as guides for adding details to the plane.
- ↱ Indicates the front edge of the piece.

PARTS LAYOUT – MiG-9

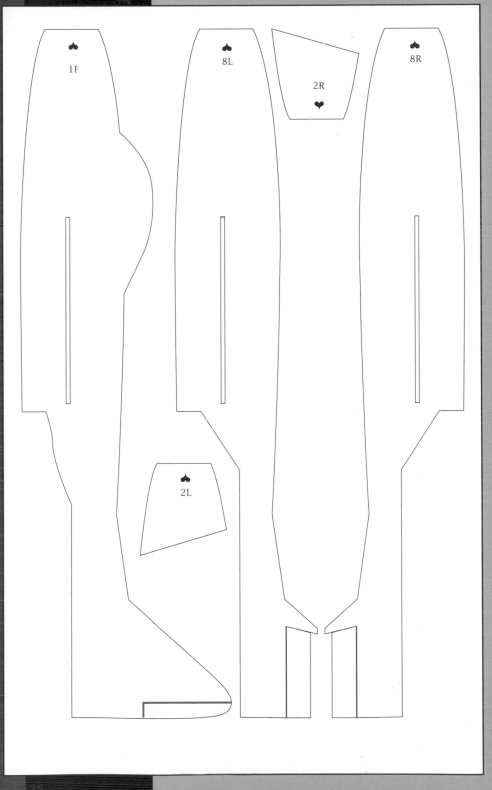

NOTE
• Cut on lines shown in black.
• Score lines in red.
• Use the blue lines as guides for adding details to the plane.
❥ Indicates the front edge of the piece.

PARTS LAYOUT – MiG-9

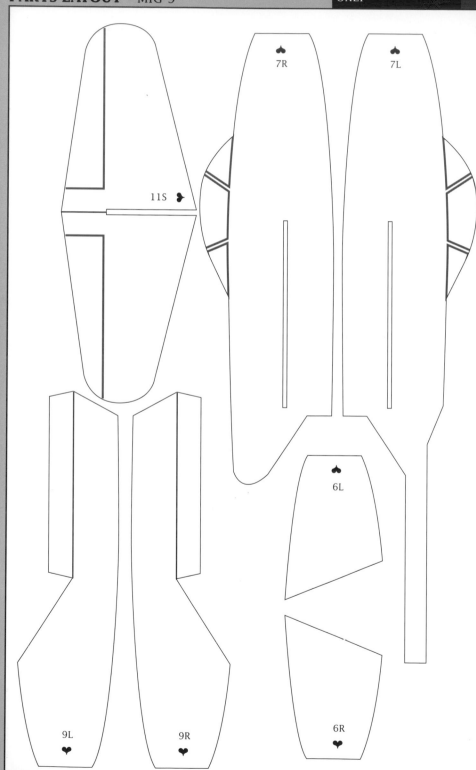

they again match their position with the lower molecules. The faster moving and more widely spaced molecules exert less pressure downward than the slower moving and more closely spaced lower molecules do upward, creating a pressure differential. The reduced pressure above the wings creates suction, much like a vacuum cleaner does. The air underneath pushes the wing into the area of reduced pressure, and the aircraft is buoyed up as it moves forward, counteracting gravity.

Second, if the leading edge of the wings is raised slightly, allowing air molecules to strike the slanted lower surface, the amount of lift generated can be

FIGURE 2
Bernoulli's Principle

In the 1770s Daniel Bernoulli discovered this law of nature: The pressure of a fluid always decreases as its rate of flow increases.

To demonstrate, hold the narrow edge of a lightweight piece of writing paper (approximately 3 x 8 in or 7.5 x 20 cm) between thumb and forefinger, letting the free end droop. Then blow over your thumb and along the paper. If done correctly the drooping end should rise because the moving air exerts less pressure downward than the still air beneath does upward. Consequently the air beneath pushes the paper upward. A lifting force has been created.

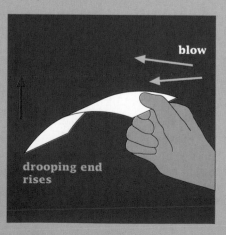

blow

drooping end rises

NOTE
• Cut on lines shown in black.
• Score lines in red.
• Use the blue lines as guides for adding details to the plane.
❥ Indicates the front edge of the piece.

increased. This slanting is called the *angle of attack*. If this angle is too steep the wing *stalls* and lift stops.

The point where all lift appears to be concentrated on a wing is called its *centre of lift* and is located at the point of maximum wing thickness about one third of the way between the leading and trailing edges.

FIGURE 3

How a wing creates lift

1. A wing increases the speed of the airflow over its upper surface so that pressure in this area is reduced. This is accomplished by making the upper wing surface curved — called camber. The distance from front to back along the curved upper surface is greater than along the lower one. Because the molecules flowing along the curve have farther to travel than the ones beneath, they increase their speed and become spaced farther apart in order to resume their former position when they leave the wing at the trailing edge. This faster moving air exerts less pressure, which means that a partial vacuum is created above the wing — suction. (By the application of Bernoulli's Principle.) The now higher pressure beneath pushes the wing upward into the vacuum, creating a lifting force. This lift acts through a point about one third of the distance between the leading and trailing edges of a wing, the point of maximum camber.

2. The lifting force can be increased if the leading edge of the wing is raised slightly. This incline is called the angle of attack. It allows the airflow to strike the lower surface. As air is deflected downward, it provides a force in the opposite direction. This additional pressure beneath the wings increases the overall lifting force. If the angle is more than about 15 degrees lift stops. The wing has stalled. Aircraft that are designed to fly at very high speeds have thin wings with only slight camber. Every wing design of any particular cross-section shape has a best angle of attack.

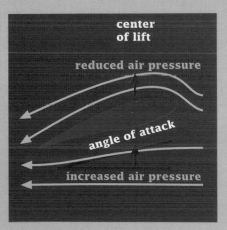

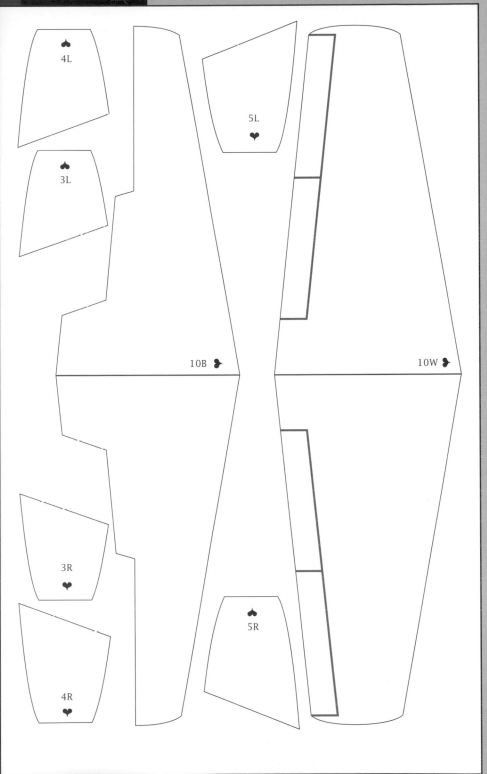

North American Aviation F-86 Sabre
the supersonic age

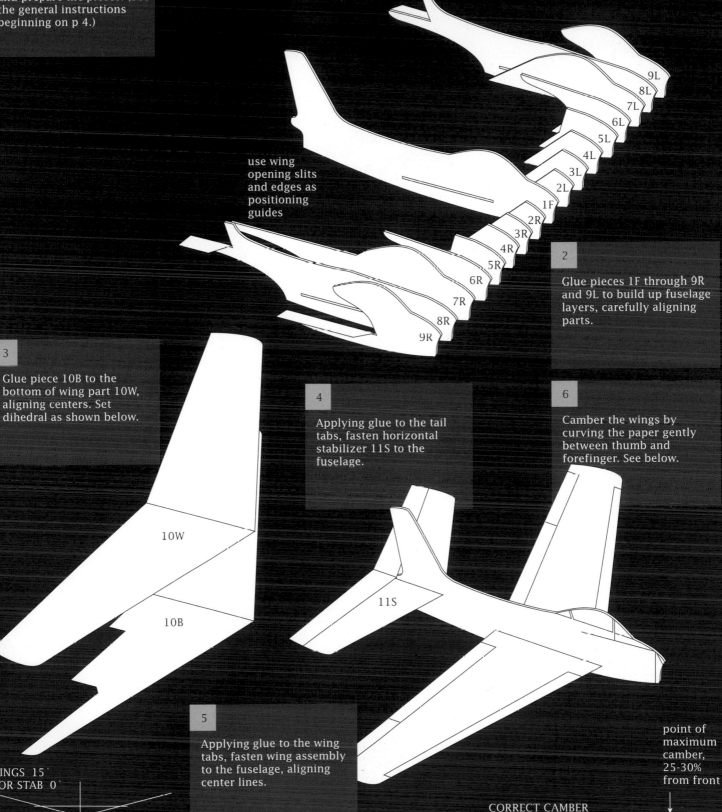

1

Photocopy the parts layouts for this model. Then cut out and prepare the pieces. (See the general instructions beginning on p 4.)

use wing opening slits and edges as positioning guides

9L
8L
7L
6L
5L
4L
3L
2L
1F
2R
3R
4R
5R
6R
7R
8R
9R

2

Glue pieces 1F through 9R and 9L to build up fuselage layers, carefully aligning parts.

3

Glue piece 10B to the bottom of wing part 10W, aligning centers. Set dihedral as shown below.

4

Applying glue to the tail tabs, fasten horizontal stabilizer 11S to the fuselage.

6

Camber the wings by curving the paper gently between thumb and forefinger. See below.

10W

10B

11S

5

Applying glue to the wing tabs, fasten wing assembly to the fuselage, aligning center lines.

WINGS 15°
HOR STAB 0°

point of maximum camber, 25-30% from front

CORRECT CAMBER

NOTE
• Cut on lines shown in black.
• Score lines in red.
• Use the blue lines as guides for adding details to the plane.
❧ Indicates the front edge of the piece.

PARTS LAYOUT – Sabre

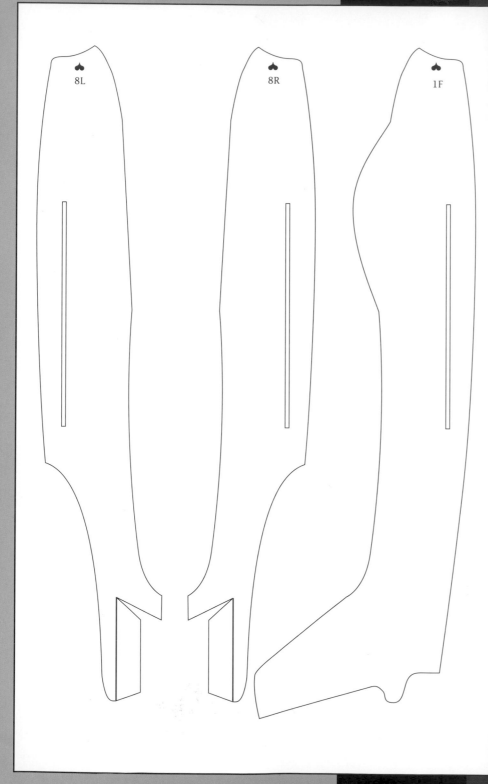

8L   8R   1F

As an aircraft is propelled forward to create lift, air molecules are pushed aside causing a certain amount of resistance. On the one hand this resistance turns into the pressure that makes lift possible; on the other hand, it becomes *drag*, which slows a plane down. The resistance of air molecules being disturbed by forward motion is called *pressure drag*. Furthermore, any surfaces on an airplane

FIGURE 4

Drag — the resisting force of air
Thrust — a propelling force

The thrust from the engine propels a plane through the air, but air resists being disturbed. This is called drag. It slows a plane down and its force increases with speed. Drag and thrust counteract each other.

At subsonic speed there are three kinds of drag: pressure drag, induced drag, and frictional drag. These combine to make up the overall drag acting on an aircraft in flight. Pressure drag is the general resistance of air to disturbance. This is what you feel when you wave your arm or run. The bigger the frontal area of an object, the greater this drag. Air always flows from an area of high pressure to an area of low pressure; therefore, in the process of generating lift, air slips around the wingtips creating a vortex. This is induced drag. Because of the relative stickiness of air, any surface of the aircraft over which air flows creates frictional drag.

For the efficient operation of aircraft, reducing drag has been a major objective in airplane design. It is called streamlining.

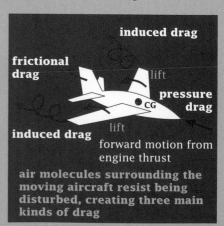

induced drag

frictional drag

lift

pressure drag

induced drag   lift

forward motion from engine thrust

air molecules surrounding the moving aircraft resist being disturbed, creating three main kinds of drag

NOTE
• Cut on lines shown in black.
• Score lines in red.
• Use the blue lines as guides for adding details to the plane.
❥ Indicates the front edge of the piece.

not parallel to the airflow add to this drag, including a wing's angle of attack and stabilizers adjusted to maintain straight and level flight.

Additionally, the pressure differential above and beneath a wing creates a vortex as air slips around the wingtip from the area of high pressure to that of low pressure. This turbulence, which always accompanies lift production, is called *induced drag*. This drag varies depending on the shape and efficiency of the wing.

Air molecules flowing over an object also tend to stick to the object's surface, adding to the air's resistance, called *frictional drag*. The smoother the surface, the less this drag is.

EFFECTS OF HIGH SPEED

The various forces combine into a general force of drag, which increases with speed. At very high speed, however, the nature of this force changes, becoming a force called *compressibility drag*. The air molecules simply cannot move aside fast enough and they begin to pile up. The air surrounding the plane begins to resemble the wake of a powerboat in water. Quite suddenly, at a certain speed, this increases the overall drag sharply. Buffeting is encountered. An airplane that was stable at a slower speed now loses its stability.

Additionally, frictional drag begins to generate heat, and the faster the speed the higher the

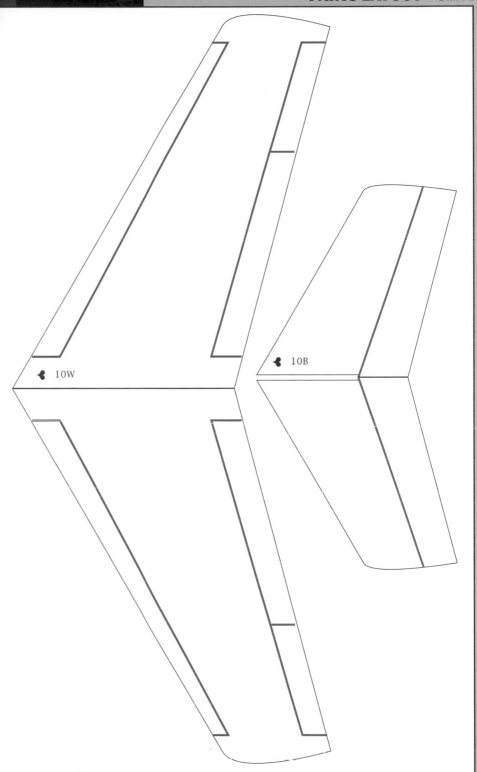

PARTS LAYOUT – Sabre

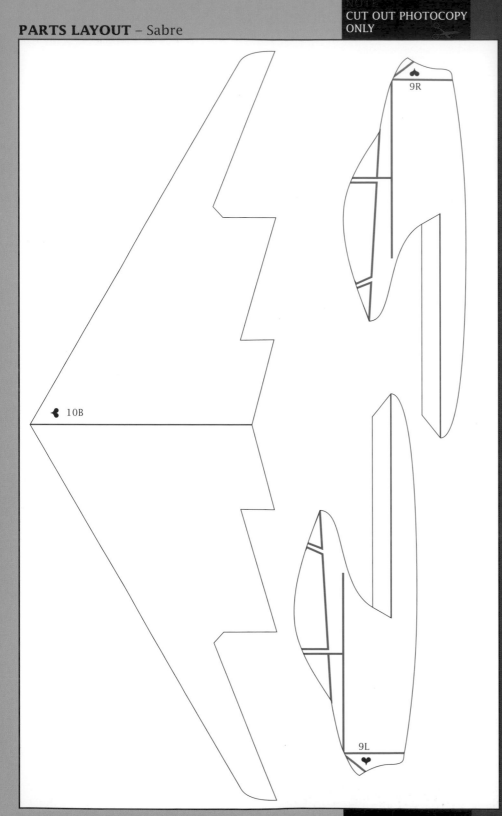

temperature becomes. For example, an airplane flying three times the speed of sound at 10,000 feet would heat up to 900 degrees F. Every material has a temperature above which it weakens and loses its usefulness. So the speed and altitude at which an airplane can travel are limited by the amount of heat its airframe can withstand, known as its *thermal barrier*.

THE SPEED OF SOUND

Sound is transmitted by pressure waves in the air. The speed at which the waves move is the speed of sound, or *sonic speed*. The speed of sound varies with air density and temperature. At sea level it is about 760 miles per hour, but is less at high altitude. Sonic speed is sometimes referred to as the *sound*

FIGURE 5

Sound and air pressure

Sound is transmitted by pressure waves in the air. The speed at which these waves travel is called sonic speed. It varies with air density and pressure. When a sound is made, such as the ringing of a bell, the waves move away in all directions. To a person nearby these pressure waves striking the ears are interpreted as the sound.

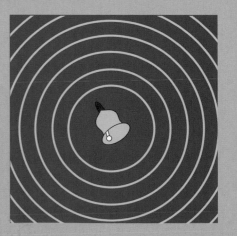

NOTE
- Cut on lines shown in black.
- Score lines in red.
- Use the blue lines as guides for adding details to the plane.
- ➜ Indicates the front edge of the piece.

CUT OUT PHOTOCOPY ONLY

PARTS LAYOUT – Sabre

barrier because the buffeting of compressibility drag made some people believe speed beyond it was impossible.

Austrian physicist, Ernst Mach, studied the action of solid objects moving through air at very high speed, and developed a method of measuring speed in terms of the speed of sound. His work was not understood for a long time, but became important as aircraft began to encounter compressibility drag as they approached the speed of sound. This speed came to be known as Mach 1, twice the speed of sound as Mach 2, and so on.

Overall shape and design deter mine the degree of stability inherent in an airplane. The stability problems of compres-sibility drag occur because an

FIGURE 6
Sound and motion

When a sound-producing object, such as an airplane, is in motion, the airplane's speed affects the spacing of its sound waves. The waves ahead of it are spaced closer together than the ones behind. The faster the airplane flies, the closer the spacing of the forward waves becomes until, at a certain speed, the airplane catches up with the waves and they can no longer move forward.

de Havilland DH-106 Comet
jet transportation begins

6

1

Photocopy the parts layouts for this model. Then cut out and prepare the pieces. (See the general instructions beginning on p 4.)

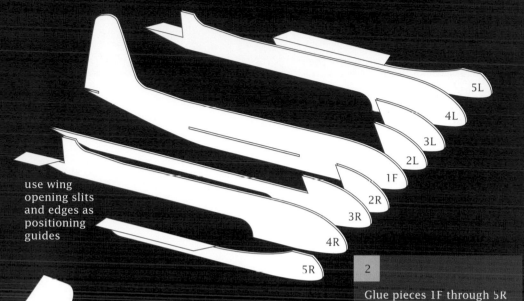

use wing opening slits and edges as positioning guides

5L
4L
3L
2L
1F
2R
3R
4R
5R

2

Glue pieces 1F through 5R and 5L to build up fuselage layers, carefully aligning parts.

3

Glue piece 6B to the bottom of wing part 6W, aligning centers. Set dihedral as shown below.

GW

6B

4

Applying glue to the tail tabs, fasten horizontal stabilizer 7S to the fuselage.

6

Camber the wings by curving the paper gently between thumb and forefinger. See below.

7S

WINGS 5°
HOR STAB 5°

5

Applying glue to the wing tabs, fasten wing assembly to the fuselage, aligning center lines.

point of maximum camber, 25-30% from front ↓

CORRECT CAMBER

PARTS LAYOUT – Comet

NOTE
CUT OUT PHOTOCOPY
ONLY

♠
4R

♠
5R

♠
1F

airplane catches up with its
own sound waves flowing
outward away from the craft.
These pressure waves interfere
with lift and stability.

FIGURE 7

Three-axis control in a standard aircraft

An aircraft in flight can rotate about its center of
gravity along three axes. (1) Its rolling motion is
controlled by ailerons in the wings. (2) Pitch is
controlled by an elevator in the horizontal
stabilizer. (3) Yaw is controlled by a rudder in the
vertical stabilizer. These are small flaps on the
trailing edges that swing back and forth like a door
on its hinges. When operated in harmony, these
controls provide equilibrium in flight — three-axis
control.

The ailerons move differentially. When one is
moved up the other goes down, and vice versa,
creating a difference in lift between the two wings
— down, lift is increased; up, lift is decreased.
This makes the aircraft roll into a banking turn to
left or right.

By moving up or down, the elevator controls the
air flowing over the horizontal stabilizer. When it
is raised the pressure over the upper surface of
the stabilizer increases, pushing downward, which
pitches the nose up as the plane rotates about the
center of gravity.

The rudder swings to left or right and keeps the
aircraft pointing straight into the airflow during
flight.

Roll stability is improved if the wings angle
upward away from the fuselage in a dihedral
angle. In level flight each wing produces the same
amount of lift. When an aircraft with dihedral is
banked, the downgoing wing's exposed surface
lengthens and its lift consequently increases,
while the upgoing wing's exposed area shortens
and its lift decreases. This lift differential causes
an opposite rolling force and the plane rights
itself, restoring equilibrium. The greater the
dihedral angle the more stable the airplane.

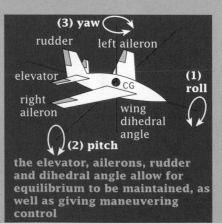

(3) yaw
rudder   left aileron
elevator   **(1) roll**
CG
right
aileron   wing
dihedral
angle
(2) pitch

the elevator, ailerons, rudder
and dihedral angle allow for
equilibrium to be maintained, as
well as giving maneuvering
control

PARTS LAYOUT – Comet

All aircraft in flight tend to be unstable in three ways: they *roll* left or right along a longitudinal axis, *pitch* nose up or down along a lateral axis running through the wings, and *yaw* from side to side around a vertical axis. To be controllable, the axes must intersect at the center of lift. The center of lift, in turn, must lie just behind the center of gravity, the balancing point where all the weight appears to be concentrated. This results in a well balanced controllable airplane.

An airplane pivots freely about this balancing point. This movement is stabilized for steady flight by some combination of *vertical* and *horizontal stabilizers*, and sometimes by wing slant, upward slightly away from the fuselage in a *dihedral*

FIGURE 8
Angle of attack and speed

Every wing is most efficient within a certain range of angle of attack and speed. With the center of gravity ahead of the center of lift, a certain amount of positive trim is always necessary to maintain a proper flight attitude. At slow speed positive trim also helps in maintaining balance despite any air turbulence. As speed is increased by adding power, the angle of attack must be decreased by the pilot to maintain level flight. The plane is retrimmed for the higher speed.

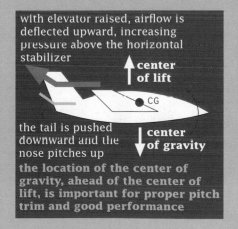

with elevator raised, airflow is deflected upward, increasing pressure above the horizontal stabilizer

center of lift

CG

the tail is pushed downward and the nose pitches up

center of gravity

the location of the center of gravity, ahead of the center of lift, is important for proper pitch trim and good performance

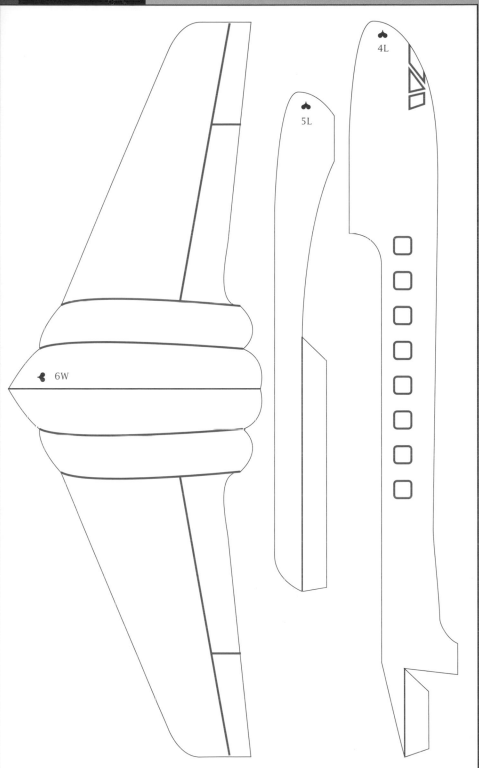

4L

5L

6W

NOTE
• Cut on lines shown in black.
• Score lines in red.
• Use the blue lines as guides for adding details to the plane.
❥ Indicates the front edge of the piece.

PARTS LAYOUT – Comet

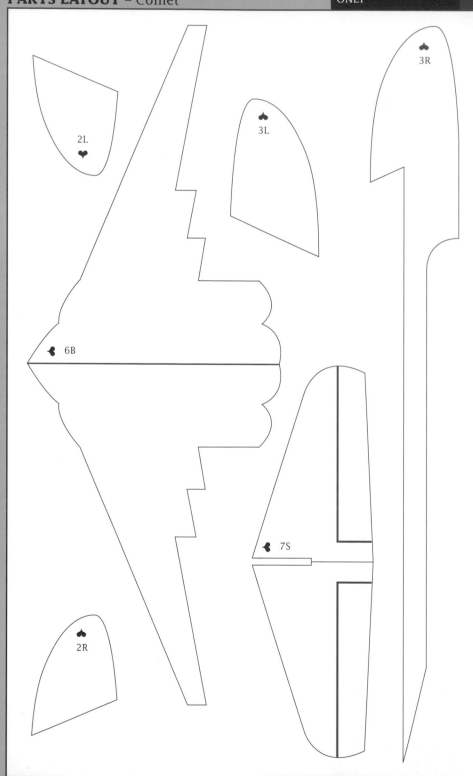

angle. Additionally, the horizontal and vertical stabilizers have small moveable surfaces *(control surfaces)* that are linked by cables and rods to stick and rudder pedals in the cockpit. By maneuvering them the pilot can make immediate adjustments and maintain equilibrium in changing conditions. The control surfaces also provide directional control for maneuvering the aircraft.

A well balanced plane can be adjusted *(trimmed)* to fly straight and level at any particular speed that the combination of airframe and propulsion system allow, requiring little pilot input. A particular angle of attack is maintained and the plane is dynamically stable.

FIGURE 9

Transonic speed and the shockwave

In their operation, wings and control surfaces produce pressure differentials. Sound waves are also pressure differentials. They move at a particular speed away from the source of the sound. As an airplane approaches sonic speed, it catches up with its own sound waves, which then no longer flow ahead of the plane (compressibility drag). A shockwave forms. This uneven airflow creates turbulence which interferes with the normal pressure differentials surrounding the airplane.

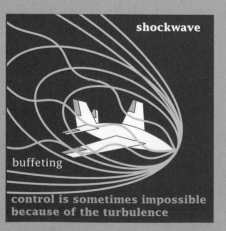

Boeing 747
jumbo transportation

1

Photocopy the parts layouts for this model. Then cut out and prepare the pieces. (See the general instructions beginning on p 4.)

6L

5L

7L

4L

3L

1F-B

use wing opening slits and edges as positioning guides

2L

1F-A

2R

6R

5R

3R

4R

7R

2

Glue pieces 1FA/1FB through 7R and 7L to build up fuselage layers, carefully aligning parts. Notice that the center fuselage piece consists of parts A & B.

3

Bring wing parts 8L and 8R together, fastening with 9T. Then glue 10L and 10R to the bottom of wing. Finally glue 11B to the very bottom. Set dihedral as shown below.

7

Camber the wings by curving the paper gently between thumb and forefinger. See below.

9T

8L

8R

10L

10R

11B

4

Glue the four engine pieces 12A through 12D, as shown.

GLUE INSIDE

12A

12B

12C

12D

13S

use engine placement guides on pp 43-44

5

Applying glue to the tail tabs, fasten horizontal stabilizer 13S to the fuselage.

point of maximum camber, 25-30% from front

6

Applying glue to the wing tabs, fasten wing assembly to the fuselage, aligning center lines. Then glue two engines to the bottom of each wing.

WINGS 10°
HOR STAB 5°

CORRECT CAMBER

NOTE
- Cut on lines shown in black.
- Score lines in red.
- Use the blue lines as guides for adding details to the plane.
- ❯ Indicates the front edge of the piece.

When an airplane flies at subsonic speed air molecules slip around the airframe smoothly and sound waves move away ahead of the airplane uneventfully. If the airplane approaches the speed of sound, called *transonic* speed, no sound waves move away ahead of it. Instead air molecules build up into a *shockwave* at the leading edges of the airplane. Because air flows at different speeds around an airplane, with different kinds of drag and various pressures, at transonic speed the turbulence surrounding the airframe is tremendous. Stabilizers and control surfaces cannot compensate for it, and the plane rolls, pitches, and yaws unpredictably.

When an airplane exeeds the speed of sound, or goes *supersonic*, the shockwave moves farther and farther back as the Mach number increases. Besides upsetting the airplane, the shockwave is heard as a loud explosion to an observer on the ground. This is the *sonic boom*, which has enough force to break windows.

Engineers knew about the kinds of difficulties experienced by pilots flying at transonic speed, and they knew that the answer to controllable supersonic flight lay in the airplane's shape. It had to be shaped and streamlined in such a way that the shockwave and its turbulent airflow were directed away from all of a plane's control surfaces. There was some guesswork involved in this, since no testing

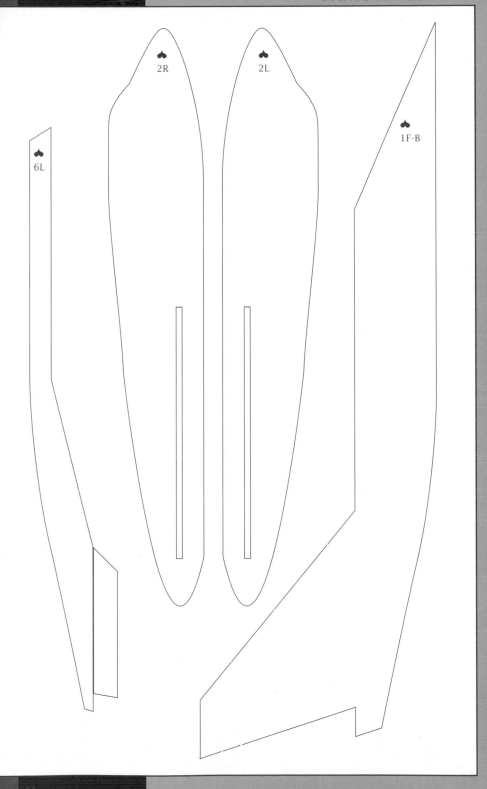

PARTS LAYOUT – 747

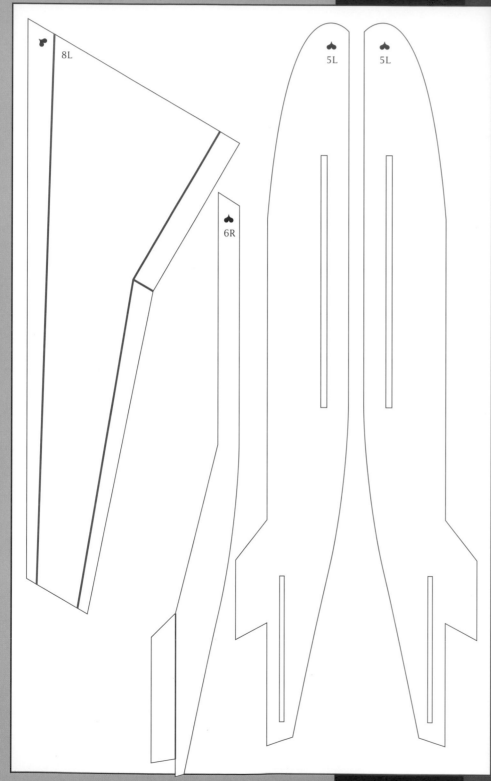

NOTE
CUT OUT PHOTOCOPY
ONLY

could be done beforehand. It was discovered quite by accident how to approach this problem practically.

SHAPE FOR SUPERSONIC FLIGHT

A wing having a low *aspect ratio* (one that is short and broad) and being very thin, was known to delay the problems of compressibility drag. The difficulty was that no one knew what particular shape to make such a wing so that at the same time it still produced lift efficiently.

After the war engineers doing research examined the He 176 and Me 262. The 262 was a twin engine design. When it was being fitted with jet en-

FIGURE 10

Supersonic speed

When an airplane flies faster than the speed of sound, airflow is once more smooth but it now has a different flow pattern. The shockwave is wedge-shaped and attached to the airplane's surfaces. It is deflected by the airplane's shape. The faster the airplane travels, the farther back the shockwave moves. For stability at high speed, the shockwave must be directed away from the plane's control surfaces at every speed. Different pressures in the shockwave are used to create lift.

smooth airflow

shockwave deflected by airplane shape

swept wings and pointed nose make a supersonic airplane stable and controllable gines, one underneath each wing, the plane's center of gravity was too far forward. In order to balance the plane the engines were moved farther back by sweeping the wings back. This swept-back design also coincidentally solved both the shape and lift problems.

Sweeping a wing back makes the wing appear to have a lower aspect ratio than it actually has. This fools the air, which now flows a longer distance diagonally across the backward-slanting surface.

Britain, leading the way in jet development after the war, built the de Havilland DH 108 Swallow, a swept wing experimental plane designed solely to go supersonic. However, in one attempt, in 1946, it unfortunately pitched wildly as it encountered compressibility drag, and broke up.

FIGURE 11
Wing sweepback

By sweeping a wing back, the air flowing across it has to travel farther than if the wing were straight. This has the effect of reducing the buffeting of compressibility drag at transonic speed.

sweepback

greater apparent distance across swept wings

swept wings reduce the effects of transonic buffeting

NOTE
• Cut on lines shown in black.
• Score lines in red.
• Use the blue lines as guides for adding details to the plane.
❥ Indicates the front edge of the piece.

CUT OUT PHOTOCOPY ONLY

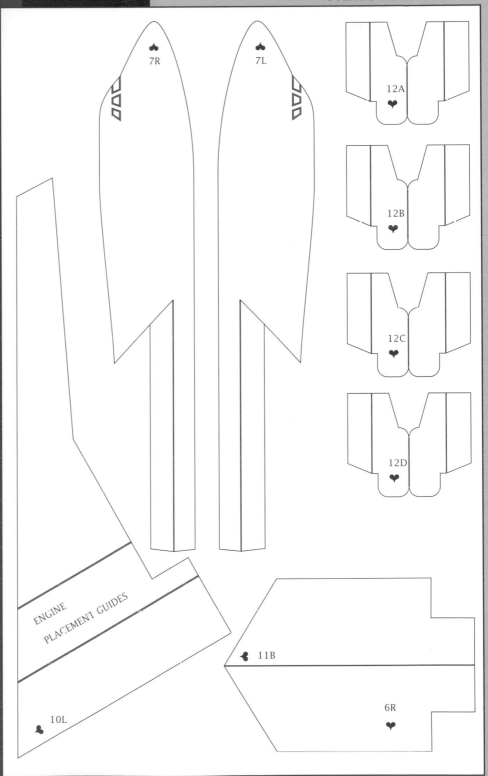

CUT OUT PHOTOCOPY ONLY

PARTS LAYOUT – 747

3L

1F-A

3R

13S

4R

4L

ENGINE PLACEMENT GUIDES

8R

9T

10R

Sweepback alone was not the answer. New and unforeseen handling problems occurred. After the Swallow's loss of control engineers were cautious in the use of swept wings until the new problems were solved.

Thereafter British designers continued to use the Gloster Meteor as a test plane for developing jet propulsion and high speed flight, pushing it ever closer to the speed of sound. They had another high speed plane under development, the de Havilland Vampire. In 1946 the Meteor held the world speed record at 613 miles per hour and the Vampire held the world altitude record at 60,000 feet. But the limits of these planes had been reached. Mach 1 remained unattained.

The British shared their knowledge with American and Russian designers during the war, and in 1942 the first American jet, the Bell Aircraft P-59 Aeracomet was powered by a British engine. This plane proved not suited to high speed and its performance was modest.

In the employ of Lockheed was a young engineer by the name of Kelly Johnson. Under his leadership, at a lab known as the Skunkworks, improvements in both airframe and jet propulsion appeared in the Lockheed P-80 Shooting Star. **(#3, p 18.)** In 1947 this jet surpassed the speed of the

Concorde SST
supersonic transportation

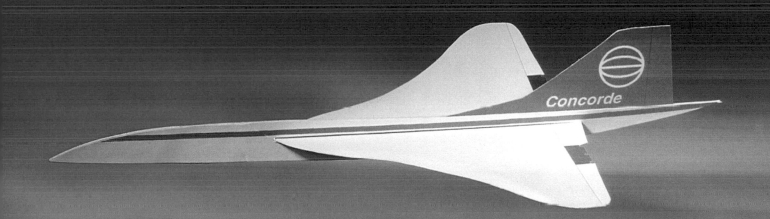

1

Photocopy the parts layouts for this model. Then cut out and prepare the pieces. (See the general instructions beginning on p 4.)

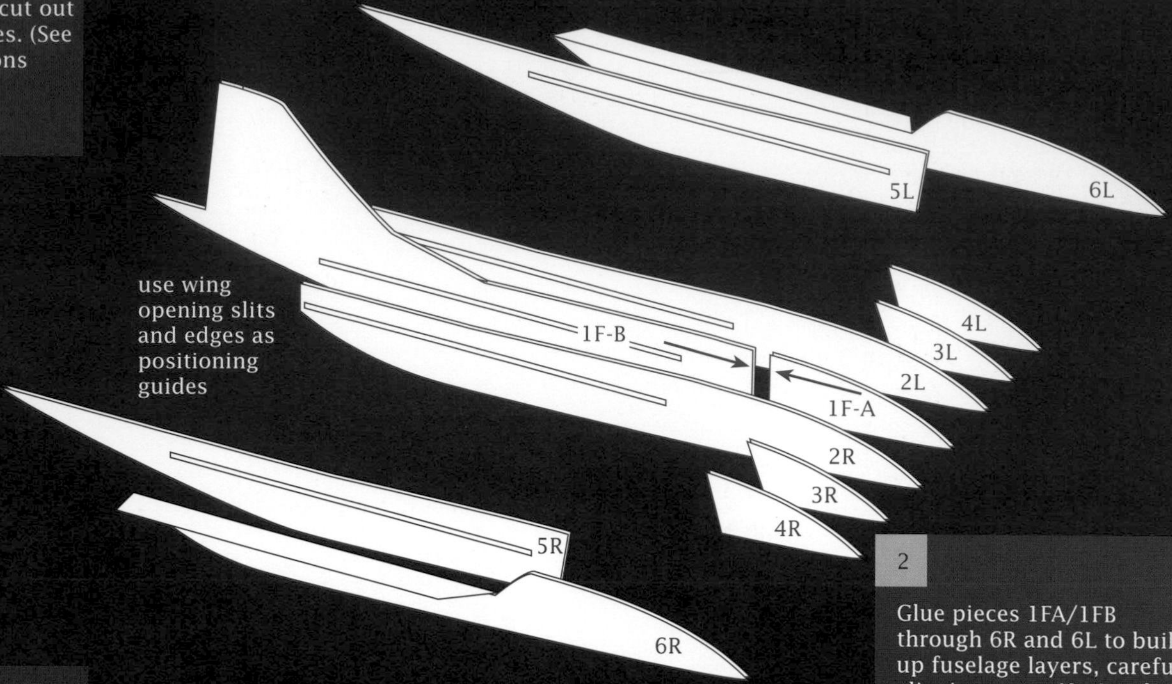

use wing opening slits and edges as positioning guides

5L

6L

4L

3L

1F-B

2L

1F-A

2R

3R

4R

2R

5R

6R

2

Glue pieces 1FA/1FB through 6R and 6L to build up fuselage layers, carefully aligning parts. Notice that the center fuselage piece consists of parts A & B.

3

Glue piece 7B to the bottom of wing part 7W, aligning centers. Set dihedral as shown below.

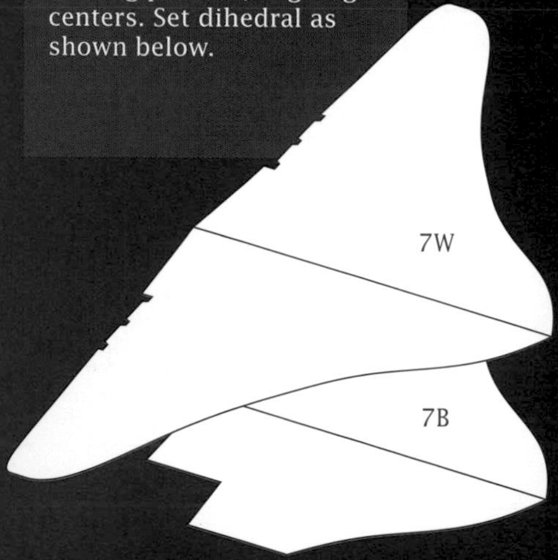

5

Camber the wings by curving the paper gently between thumb and forefinger. See below.

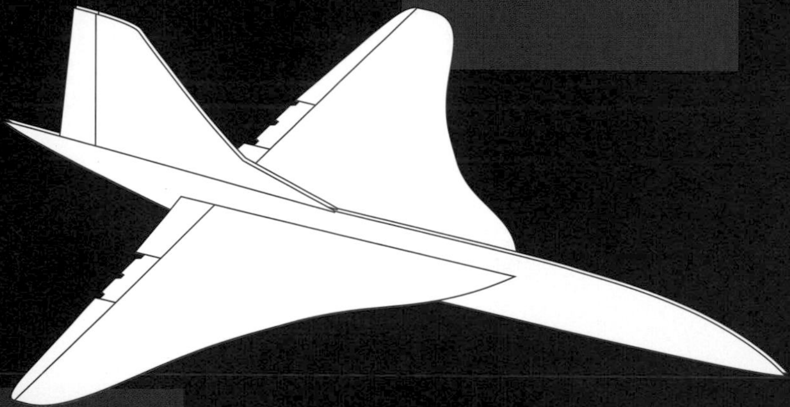

7W

7B

4

Applying glue to the wing tabs, fasten wing assembly to the fuselage, aligning center lines.

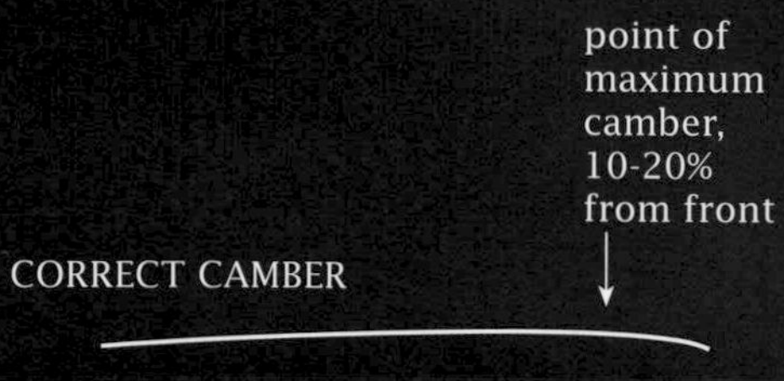

WINGS 3

point of maximum camber, 10-20% from front

CORRECT CAMBER

PARTS LAYOUT – Concorde

Meteor by flying 623 miles per hour and bringing the world speed record to the United States. The Shooting Star had a slender fuselage with thin tapered wings. The plane proved to be a very good design for subsonic flight and was developed into a jet trainer as the T-33 which, after 50 years, is still used in some countries.

The year 1947 was a breakthrough year. The American Douglas Skystreak exceeded the Shooting Star's record, pushing it to 650 miles per hour. That plane also exceeded the Vampire's altitude record by flying to 75,000 feet. Aircraft designers knew that Mach 1 was just around the corner.

For the next supersonic attempt the simple rocket engine was again called into service. The plane was the American Bell X-1. Its wings were not swept, but short, tapered, and very thin, a design thought to be suitable. Because the shape of the fuselage also determines airflow, this plane was shaped like a 50-calibre bullet, which was known to be stable at supersonic speed. Powered by a four-chamber rocket engine, the X-1 was carried to altitude in the bomb bay of a Boeing B-29 Superfortress, then released and fired up. After a number of flights into the dangerous transonic range, each faster than the one before, this plane attained 670 miles per hour at 42,000 feet, or Mach 1.2. It was a success. The date was October 14, 1947, one year after the ill fated Swallow attempt.

PARTS LAYOUT – Concorde

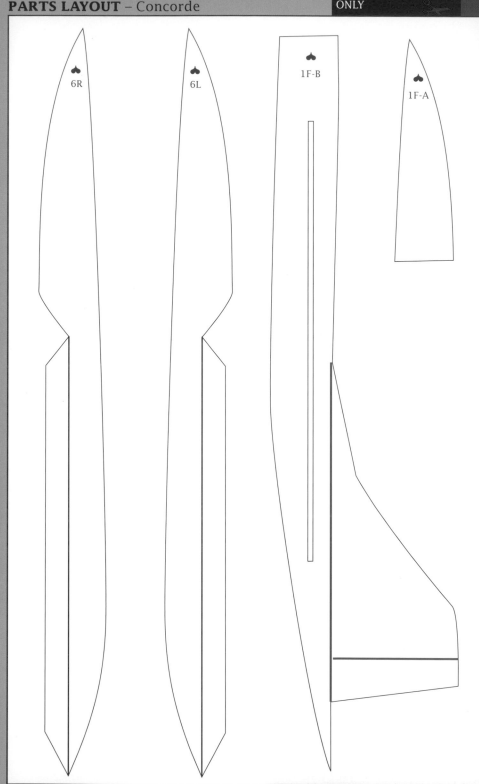

Research into wing sweepback continued by various airframe designers. North American Aviation took the lead in its development, but the Mikoyan-Gurevich company in Russia was close behind.

Russia had not actively developed jet propulsion during the war, but at war's end experimented by replacing the piston engine and propeller in a wartime Yak 3 with a captured German jet engine. Soon thereafter, in 1946, the Mikoyan-Gurevich company produced the first all-Russian jet, the MiG-9. **(#4, p 23.)** It was of conventional design without swept wings and subsonic, matching the Meteor in performance. But by 1950 this company had developed a swept wing supersonic machine, the MiG-15. In the Korean War it did battle with the American F-86 Sabre, with which it was closely matched. **(#5, p 28.)**

The swept wing F-86 Sabre and the MiG-15 had been in the planning stages when the Swallow crashed. In these planes the new handling problems of swept wings were identified and solved.

When the first model of the Sabre was released, also in 1947, it flew at just subsonic speed in level flight, and went supersonic successfully in a dive. Models produced from 1950 on were supersonic in level flight, although only in short bursts using an *after-*

NOTE
• Cut on lines shown in black.
• Score lines in red.
• Use the blue lines as guides for adding details to the plane.
➤ Indicates the front edge of the piece.

burner (see p 76). This very successful airplane, the first supersonic fighter, was built in large numbers and remained in active service for the next twenty-five years in different countries. Many pilots said it was the best plane they ever flew.

The American X-1 experiments had proved that supersonic flight was a possibility, and the F-86 Sabre and the MiG-15 made it practical. In the meantime other countries, such as Italy and France, had also begun jet research, introducing successful models in the 1950s.

Jet propulsion changed the shape of the airplane through a very practical necessity, resulting in clean, gracefully swept lines of extraordinary beauty, exemplified first in the Sabrejet. Thereafter these lines, together with the futuristic whine of turbines and roar flames characterized a new generation of powered flight.

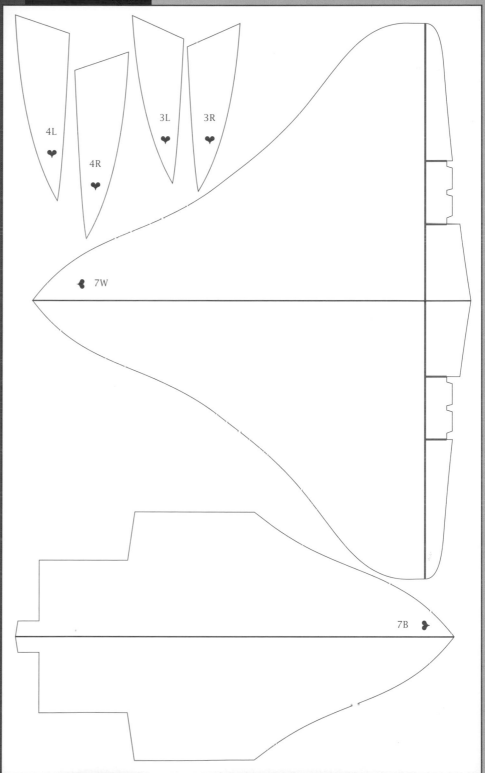

Airbus A310
fat-bodied airliner

1

Photocopy the parts layouts for this model. Then cut out and prepare the pieces. (See the general instructions beginning on p 4.)

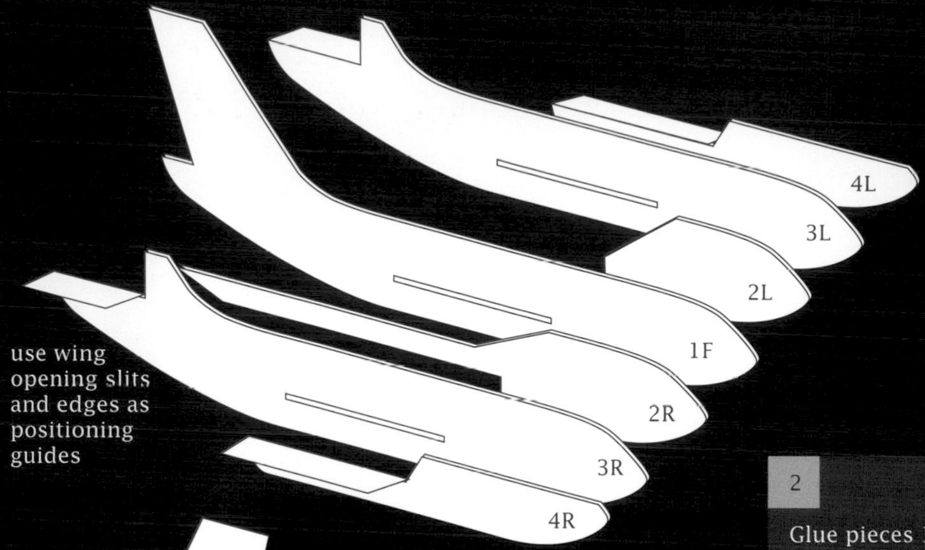

use wing opening slits and edges as positioning guides

4L
3L
2L
1F
2R
3R
4R

2

Glue pieces 1F through 4R and 4L to build up fuselage layers, carefully aligning parts.

3

Bring wing parts 5L and 5R together, fastening with 6T. Then glue 7L and 7R to the bottom of wing. Finally glue 8B to the very bottom. Set dihedral as shown below.

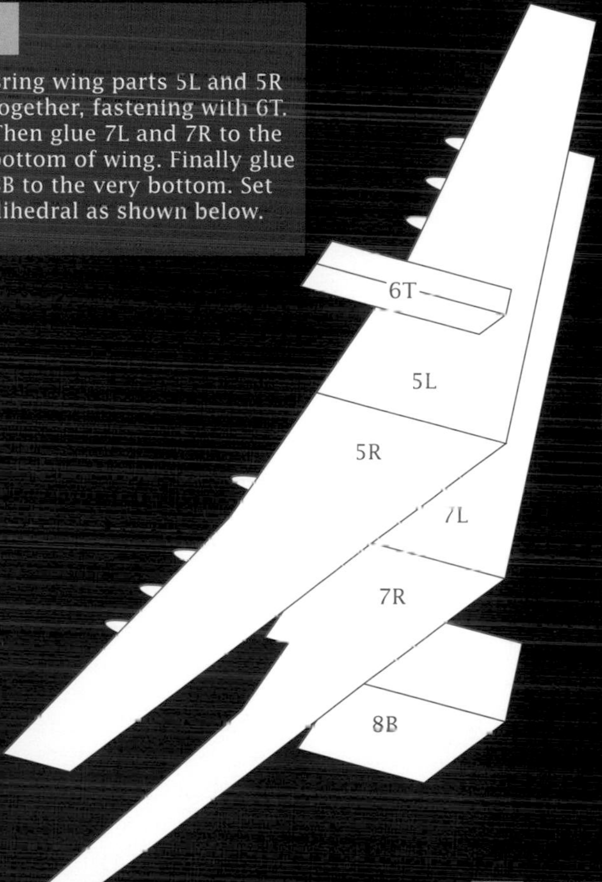

4

Glue the two engine pieces 9A and 9B, as shown.

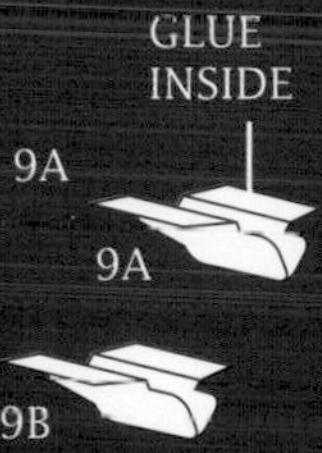

GLUE INSIDE

9A

9B

7

Camber the wings by curving the paper gently between thumb and forefinger. See below.

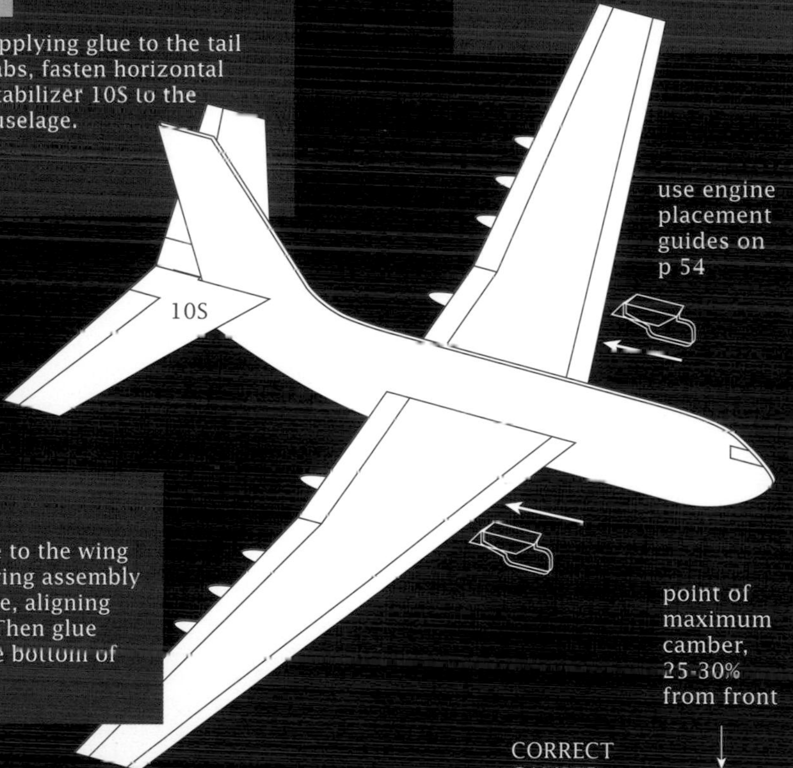

6T

5L

5R

7L

7R

8B

5

Applying glue to the tail tabs, fasten horizontal stabilizer 10S to the fuselage.

use engine placement guides on p 54

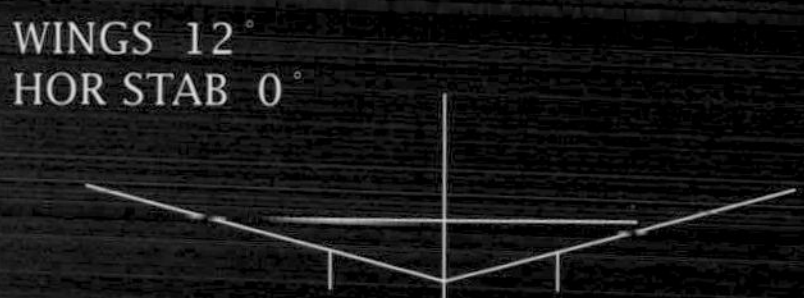

10S

6

Applying glue to the wing tabs, fasten wing assembly to the fuselage, aligning center lines. Then glue engines to the bottom of wings.

point of maximum camber, 25-30% from front

WINGS 12°
HOR STAB 0°

CORRECT CAMBER

NOTE
• Cut on lines shown in black.
• Score lines in red.
• Use the blue lines as guides for adding details to the plane.
❧ Indicates the front edge of the piece.

PARTS LAYOUT – Airbus

NOTE
CUT OUT PHOTOCOPY
ONLY

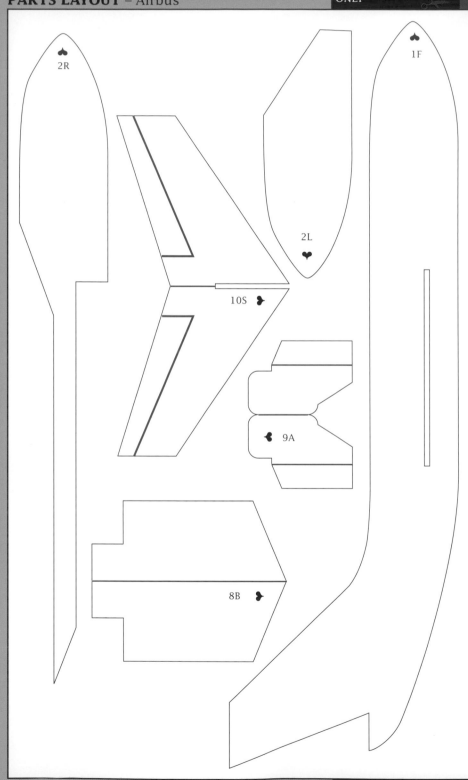

jet transportation

Although all jets are powerful, not all are meant to go supersonic, and not all are fighters. Transport airplane performance had followed military airplane performance since the beginning of flight by the Wright brothers. And now, because of the efficiency of jet propulsion, jet engines were used in many different kinds of subsonic transport planes. During the 1950s airports everywhere increasingly displayed a variety of them.

When prosperity returned in the 1950s an increasing number of people traveled by air. Large piston driven four-engined airliners, modeled on wartime heavy bombers, were built to accommodate them. At 300 miles per hour, a plane flying from New York to Los Angeles could complete the trip the same day. Even Europe was available with next-day arrival times. These airliners proved that passengers could be carried safely for great distances at high speed and at an altitude above the turbulence of weather. Pressurized cabins provided the comfort of ground-level breathing in the thin air of high altitude. With these American-built planes, airlines established worldwide routes and set the stage for jet powered transportation.

Not to be outdone by American companies, the British took the next step. In 1952, on

PARTS LAYOUT – Airbus

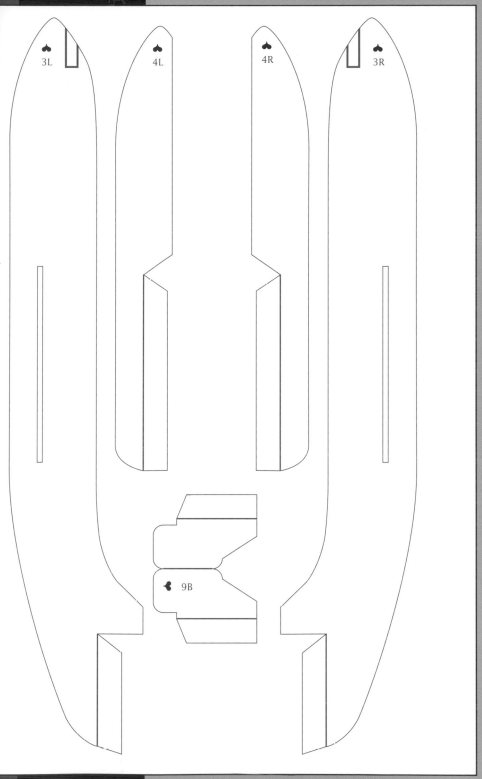

the London-to-Johannesburg route, a new sleek airliner was introduced, the de Havilland DH-106 Comet. **(#6, p 34.)** It was a sensation. This airliner provided non-stop, quiet, comfortable, 500-miles-per-hour-service at 40,000 feet. However, Britain's first step into jet transportation came at a high price.

With its four turbojet engines hidden in the gracefully swept wings, the smooth-skinned Comet had a promising futuristic look. Because it was nearly 200 miles per hour faster than its nearest competitor, as many as ten different airlines immediately ordered Comets. But in two short years the Comets were all grounded. Several had mysteriously broken up in midair, with great loss of life. The Comets' airframes could not withstand prolonged pressurization at high altitudes. They cracked around the windows and came apart.

All was not lost for the Comet, however, for it has come back into service as an entirely different airplane, the Nimrod. It is used by the Royal Airforce in long-range maritime patrol. The plane's electronic surveillance hardware and weaponry mask its once graceful lines. It is now one of the world's most advanced anti-submarine aircraft and will be in service well into the next century.

The Boeing company, known for its successful bombers, began experiments with jet engines in 1947. As did the Me 262,

NOTE
• Cut on lines shown in black.
• Score lines in red.
• Use the blue lines as guides for adding details to the plane.
❯ Indicates the front edge of the piece.

PARTS LAYOUT – Airbus

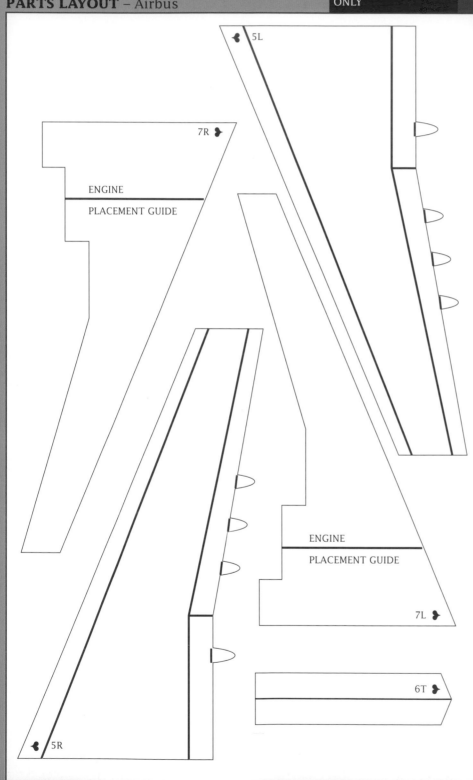

Boeing's planes had the engines suspended in pods beneath gracefully swept wings. With their experimental XB-47 bomber, they had discovered that this arrangement yielded extraordinary results for large airplanes. With its six podded jet engines spread along the wings, the XB-47 could fly 600 miles per hour at 45,000 feet, making it virtually immune from attack. This design, more than any other, inspired all future jet powered swept-wing transports.

In 1954, just before the Comet airliner crashes, Boeing introduced the first American jet airliner, the 707. After the Comets were grounded, the Boeing 707, along with transports introduced by other manufacturers, such as the Douglas DC-8, took the lead as the world's airliners.

These airliners cruised at 550 miles per hour at 40,000 feet. They were quiet and comfortable, and brought great change to the fabric of society as they seriously challenged train and ship travel. Now, transcontinental and transoceanic flights became commonplace. Air travel was no longer just for the wealthy.

With these planes a standard was set that remains to this day. Although airliners today can fly at 625 miles per hour, they rarely do so in regular service. To go faster is to enter the transonic range where more power is required and fuel

Avro Arrow
futuristic fifties

1

Photocopy the parts layouts for this model. Then cut out and prepare the pieces. (See the general instructions beginning on p 4.)

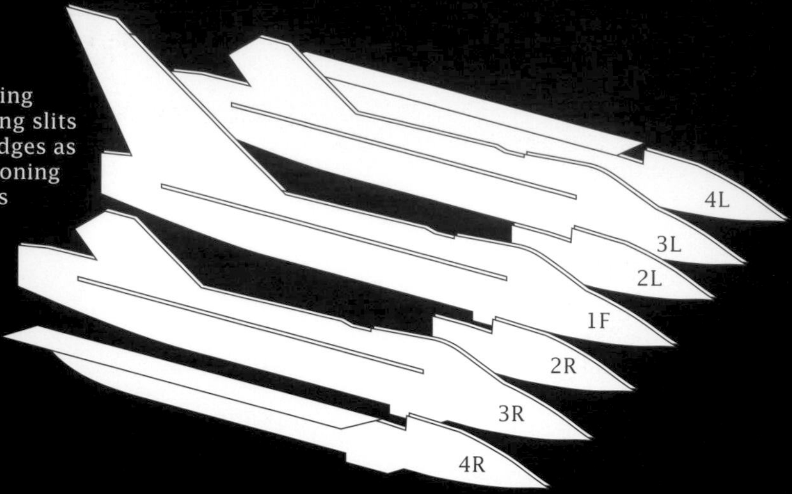

use wing opening slits and edges as positioning guides

4L
3L
2L
1F
2R
3R
4R

3

Glue piece 5B to the bottom of wing part 5W, aligning centers. Set dihedral as shown below.

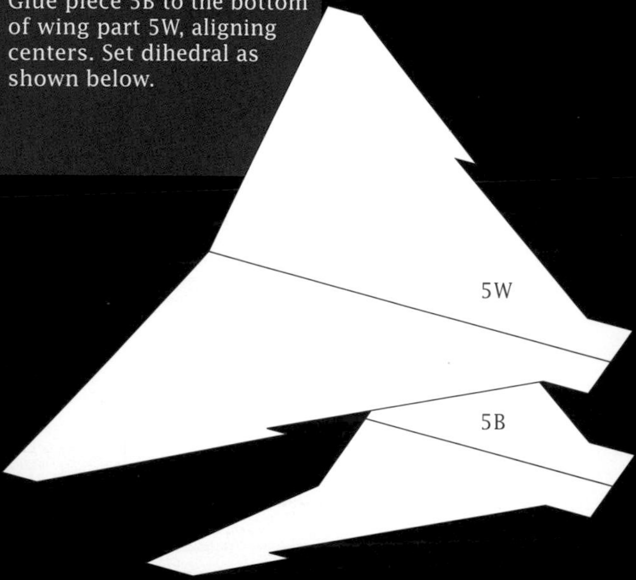

5W

5B

2

Glue pieces 1F through 4R and 4L to build up fuselage layers, carefully aligning parts.

6

Camber the wings by curving the paper gently between thumb and forefinger. See below.

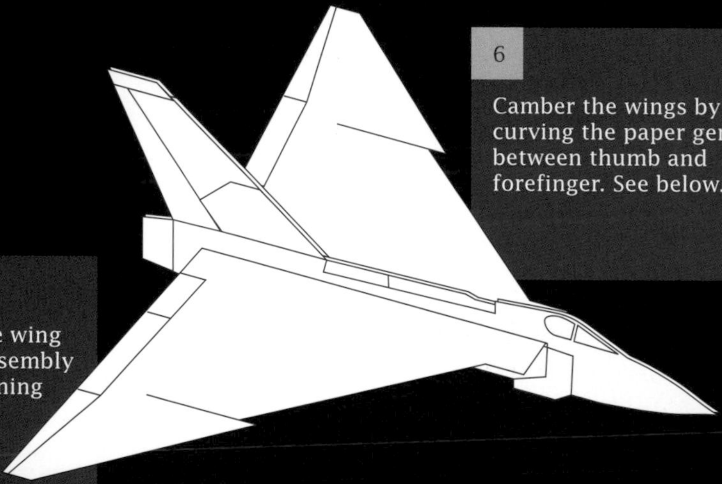

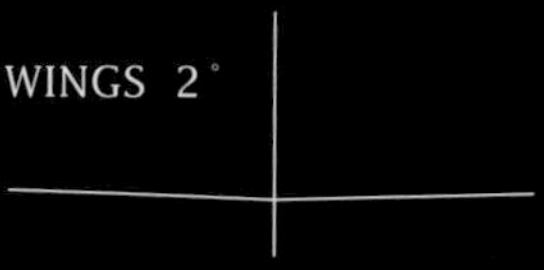

5

Applying glue to the wing tabs, fasten wing assembly to the fuselage, aligning center lines.

WINGS 2°

point of maximum camber, 10-20% from front

CORRECT CAMBER

NOTE
• Cut on lines shown in black.
• Score lines in red.
• Use the blue lines as guides for adding details to the plane.
⬥ Indicates the front edge of the piece.

NOTE
CUT OUT PHOTOCOPY
ONLY

PARTS LAYOUT – Arrow

consumption increases sharply because of compressibility drag, and there are added stability problems. Taking into account the total time required for boarding, departure, and arrival procedures, airspeed would have to increase greatly in order to shorten travel time.

As the throng of passengers and loads of cargo increased, manufacturers ventured to build bigger and bigger transports instead of faster ones. One such giant is the Boeing 747 Jumbo, first seen by the public in 1968 as it entered service on long-haul passenger routes. **(#7, p 39.)** It is characterized by its wide body. Originally this design had been intended for military cargo transport, but Boeing lost the military contract to the Lockheed company and its design, the C5 Galaxy.

The 747 Jumbo carries almost 500 passengers. It is powered by four fanjet engines, (see p 79) which combine propeller and jet propulsion. They are more fuel efficient and operate more quietly than ordinary turbojets. With a nonstop range of nearly 7000 miles, the New York-to-Tokyo route, once a month-long ocean voyage or a five-day piston-powered air journey, became an overnight trip. The 747 is popular on many regular and holiday transoceanic charter routes. For many people it is their first jet encounter, as they go on family vacations.

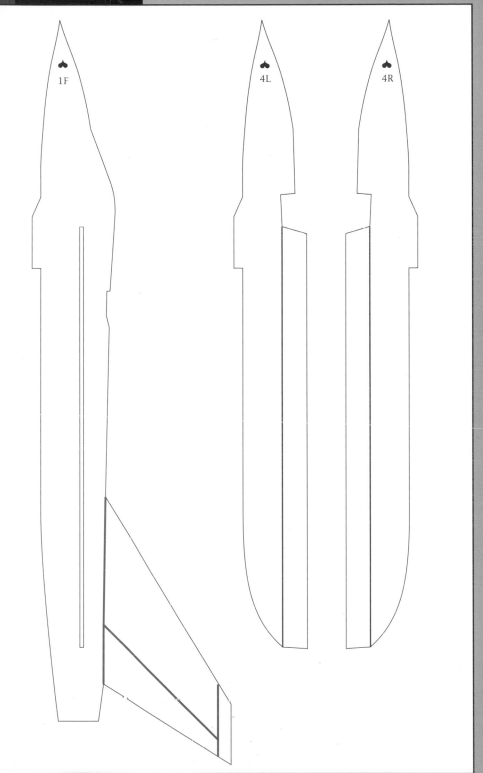

PARTS LAYOUT – Arrow

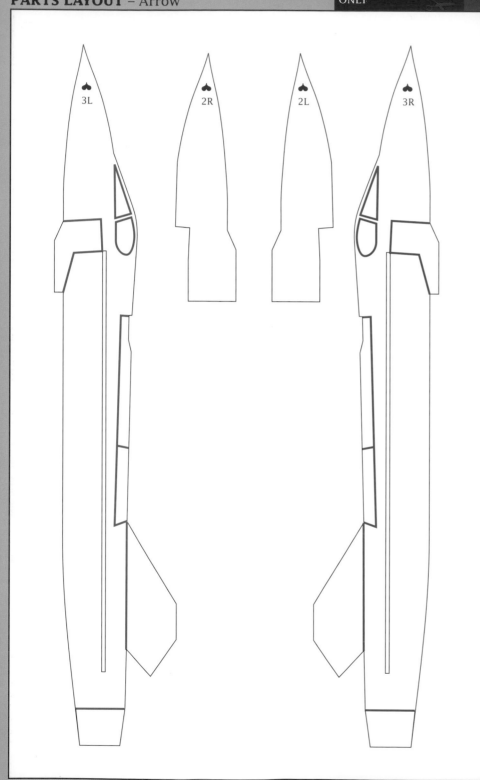

As businesses prospered in the 1950s, busy executives traveled the world. Their time was valuable and they demanded speedier flights. This need for speed affected the design of airliners, as the need for speed had fighters. Engineers began to investigate the possibility of supersonic transportation. Building any aircraft is a costly venture, which affects the cost of air travel. The goal was to reduce the time of air travel from Europe to North America to three hours, and make travel between any cities in the world a possibility within a twelve hour period, no matter the cost.

With this in mind, in 1962, British and French engineers collaborated to produce the Concorde. **(#8, p 45.)** Rolls-Royce developed engines with enough thrust to propel this airliner through the air at a sustained supersonic speed, which is known as *super-cruise.* The Concorde is made of aluminum alloy, which has a thermal barrier of Mach 2, a speed that nicely fit the travel time objectives. Electronic devices aid the pilot to fly and navigate the airplane. This beautiful stiletto whisks its passengers across the ocean at twice the speed of sound in first class luxury. The plane's success, however, is limited, first by cost of this luxury, and second by the fact that it cannot go supersonic over populated areas because of the effects of the sonic boom.

NOTE
• Cut on lines shown in black.
• Score lines in red.
• Use the blue lines as guides for adding details to the plane.
❥ Indicates the front edge of the piece.

PARTS LAYOUT – Arrow

By the 1970s ordinary travelers could travel easily to any city in the world. Unlike the business executive, however, they wanted to do it cheaply. This led to the design of an entirely different sort of airliner, the Airbus. **(# 9, p 50.)** The name alone suggests economy. This plane is a collaboration between France, Germany, Holland, Spain, Britain, and others.

The Airbus, a smaller wide-bodied airliner with 330 seats, economized in two ways. First, the way in which pilots controlled the plane had always been achieved through mechanical linkages between the cockpit and the control surfaces. Guages and other instruments were traditionally also mechanical. Advances in electronics and computers had occurred, in part, through lessons learned in building military planes. This gave designers enough confidence in computers to replace mechanical devices with electronic ones in passenger planes. This simplified the airplane and made it more economical to operate. Second, large jet airliners had usually had four engines, but with improvements in the power output and durability of fanjets, only two were used on the Airbus. This meant further economy.

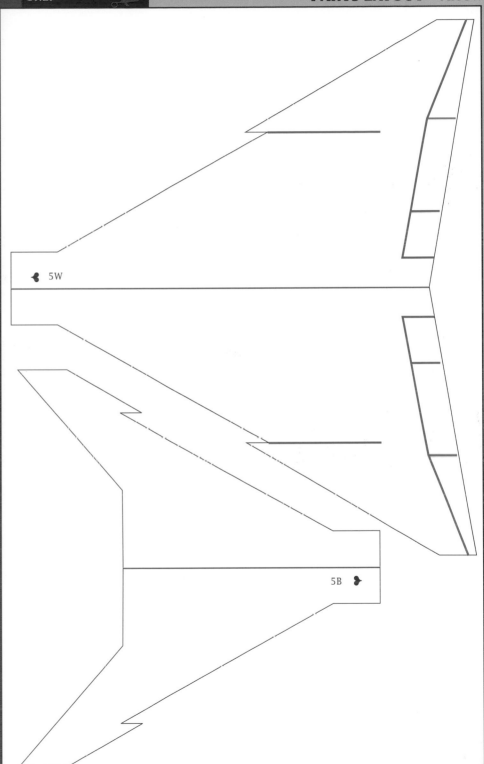

General Dynamics F-16 Falcon
airborne computer

1

Photocopy the parts layouts for this model. Then cut out and prepare the pieces. (See the general instructions beginning on p 4.)

2

Glue pieces 1F through 5R and 5L to build up fuselage layers, carefully aligning parts.

notice that fuselage parts 6L and 6R are not glued in place until the horizontal stabilizer and wings are in place

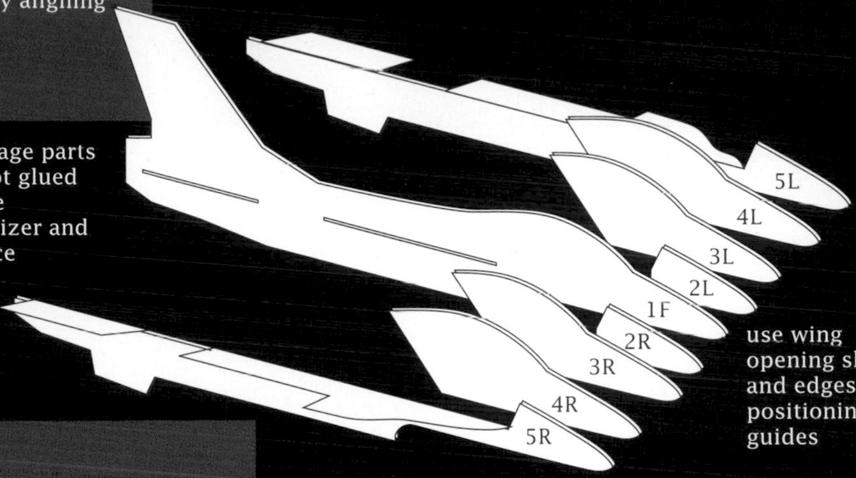

5L
4L
3L
2L
1F
2R
3R
4R
5R

use wing opening slits and edges as positioning guides

3

Glue piece 7B to the bottom of wing part 7W, aligning centers. For added strength, apply glue and bend over wingtips. Set dihedral as shown below.

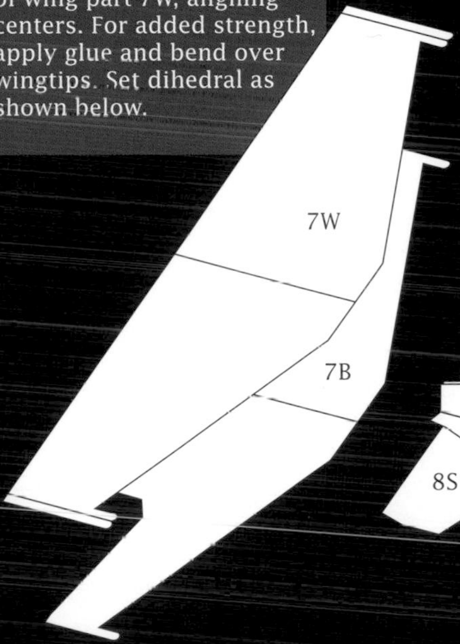

4

Applying glue to tail tabs, fasten horizontal stabilizer 8S to the fuselage.

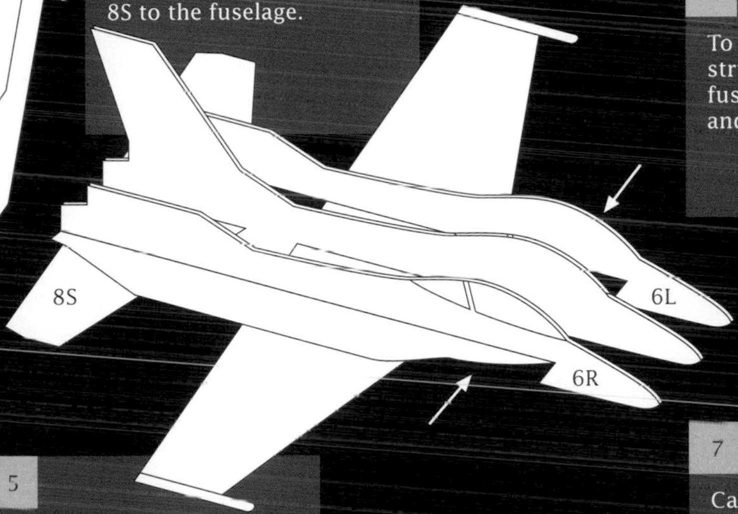

6

To finish the plane's structure, apply glue to fuselage pieces 6L and 6R and press into position.

7W

7B

8S

6L

6R

5

Applying glue to the wing tabs, fasten wing assembly to the fuselage, aligning center lines.

7

Camber the wings by curving the paper gently between thumb and forefinger. See below.

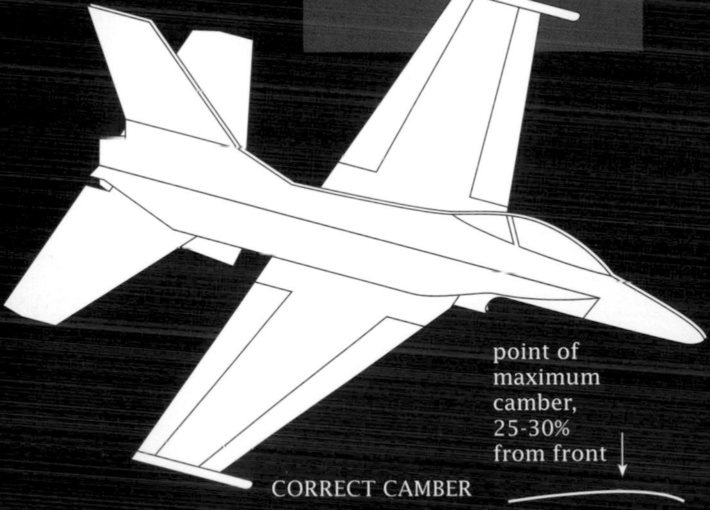

WINGS 10°
HOR STAB -10°

point of maximum camber, 25-30% from front ↓

CORRECT CAMBER

NOTE
• Cut on lines shown in black.
• Score lines in red.
• Use the blue lines as guides for adding details to the plane.
❥ Indicates the front edge of the piece.

PARTS LAYOUT – Falcon

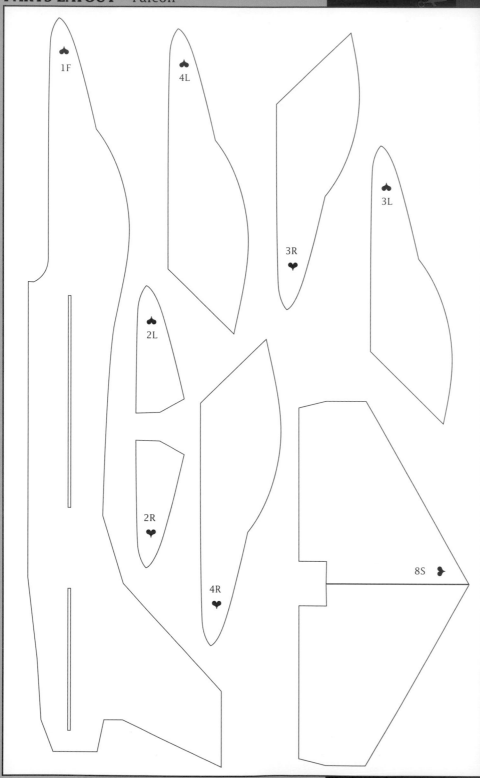

jet develop- ment

The extensive use of electronics did not originate in the Airbus. Neither did supercruise capability orginate with the Concorde. Both had their origin in the Canadian Avro Arrow, an aircraft on which development began in 1952. **(#10, p 55.)** The plane was designed as an interceptor to defend the vast Canadian north. For this role it had to be capable of supersonic speed at high altitude for its entire flight. Supersonic research in Britain and the United States provided basic knowledge for the construction of this all-aluminum alloy aircraft. Five Arrows had been built and test flown before the program was halted for political reasons in 1958.

The Arrow's external surface was completely smooth and it carried all its stores, such as fuel, weapons, and electronic devices internally. It had steeply swept delta (triangular) wings and no horizontal stabilizer. To avoid pitch-up problems in such wings, each wing had a notch in its leading edge. The sleek plane was designed for a speed of Mach 3, a speed in excess of its thermal barrier. This meant it had to have air conditioners to keep its skin cool.

The Arrow was the first plane to be controlled electronically (*fly-by-wire*). In this system wires run to small motors that move the control surfaces instead of mechanical linkages.

Its navigation and guidance systems were also entirely electronic. The idea was to have an airplane that could fly and do battle entirely by itself, computer controlled, with only the pilot keeping an eye on things. Computer control was necessary because to maneuver at speeds in excess of Mach 2 requires quick response beyond human capability. This experimental plane was twenty years ahead of its time and influenced future developments in aircraft design.

One plane to benefit from fly-by-wire control and electronic systems research was the General Dynamics F-16 Falcon, developed in the 1970s. **(#11, p 60.)** This lightweight, high-speed, and maneuverable fighter was in some ways to fighters what the Airbus was to transports – simple and economical. Like the Arrow, it is completely electronic in its controls and systems. Unlike the Arrow, its airframe is made mainly of lightweight plastic composites instead of metal. These materials are very strong, making the airplane virtually indestructable under the conditions of high-speed maneuvers.

The Falcon introduced a new shape to jets. It has clipped delta wings with a tail and ventral fins. The wings are smoothly blended into the fuselage with *strakes*, which are long leading edge extensions. The entire fuselage- strake-wing combination produces lift. With its large "shark's mouth" air inlet beneath the cockpit, it appears

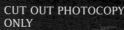

NOTE
- Cut on lines shown in black.
- Score lines in red.
- Use the blue lines as guides for adding details to the plane.
- ➧ Indicates the front edge of the piece.

CUT OUT PHOTOCOPY ONLY

PARTS LAYOUT – Falcon

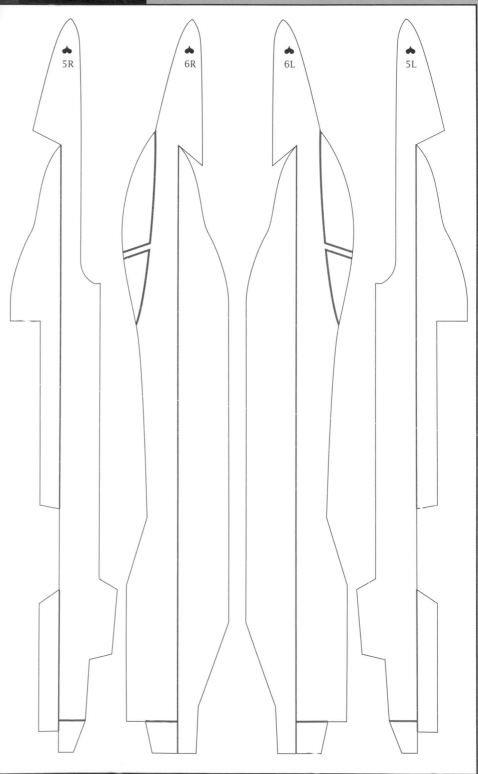

NOTE

- Cut on lines shown in black.
- Score lines in red.
- Use the blue lines as guides for adding details to the plane.
- ❯ Indicates the front edge of the piece.

PARTS LAYOUT – Falcon

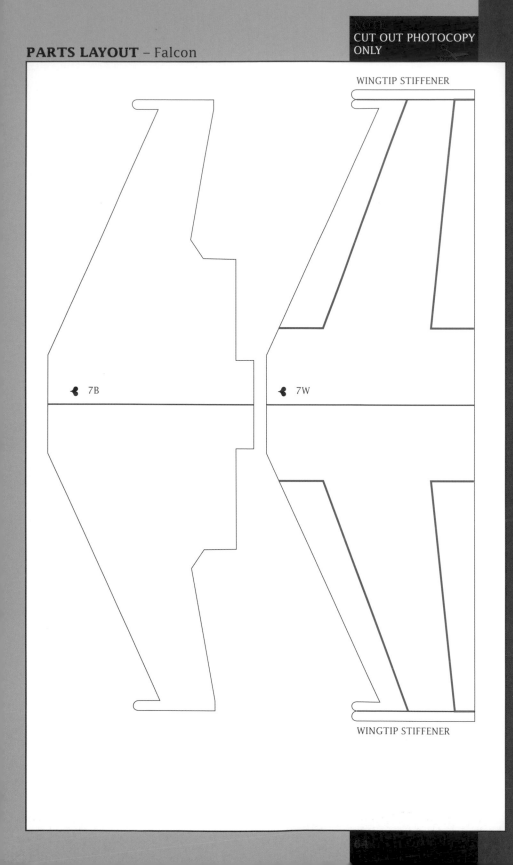

WINGTIP STIFFENER

7B

7W

WINGTIP STIFFENER

as though the plane is perched on top of its single turbojet engine. It flies at supersonic speed for short bursts using an afterburner This agile fighter is used by the air forces of many countries.

The new integrated airframe shape is also used in other fighters. One is the Russian MiG-29 Fulcrum, which came into service in 1985. **(#12, p 65.)** It belongs to a class of heavy multi-task fighters built by various countries. All are closely matched in performance.

This plane has twin vertical stabilizers, and the air inlets for its two large turbojet engines are beneath the fuselage. It has a rugged landing gear for operation using rough airstrips. It uses extensive electronics in its various systems, but has mechanical control links. The MiG-29, built partly of plastic composites, flies in excess of Mach 2 in short bursts, using afterburners.

This plane can out-maneuver many of its competitors because its jet nozzles can be angled to direct thrust in different directions, called *thrust vectoring.* See p 81. This capability was introduced by the Hawker Harrier in the late 1960s. In that plane thrust vectoring allowed for vertical take off and hovering. Thrust vectoring will be used increasingly in the future.

Mikoyan MiG-29 Fulcrum
super maneuverability

12

1

Photocopy the parts layouts for this model. Then cut out and prepare the pieces. (See the general instructions beginning on p 4.)

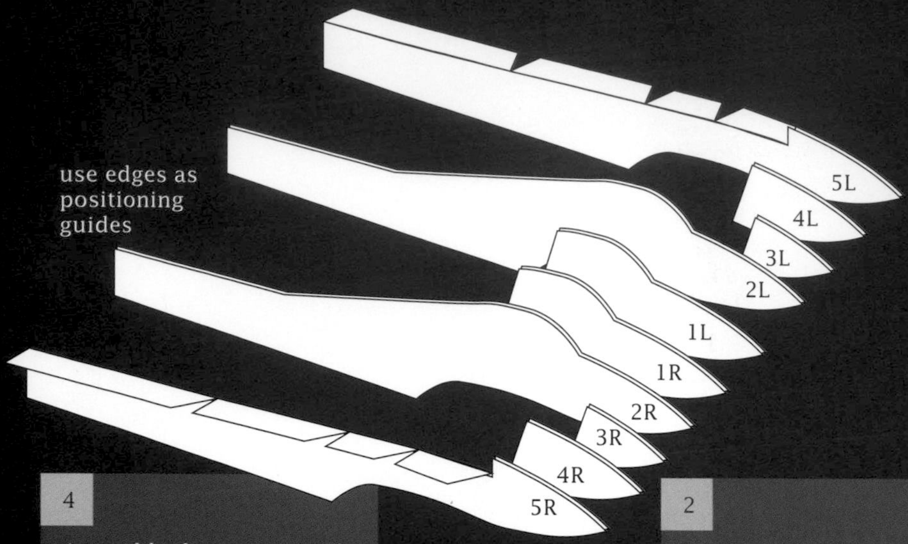

use edges as positioning guides

5L
4L
3L
2L
1L
1R
2R
3R
4R
5R

3

Bring wing parts 6L and 6R together. Glue piece 6B to the bottom, aligning centers. Set dihedral as shown below.

4

Assemble the two vertical stabilizers. First apply glue to 7J and attach to 7L. Then apply glue to 7K and attach to 7R.

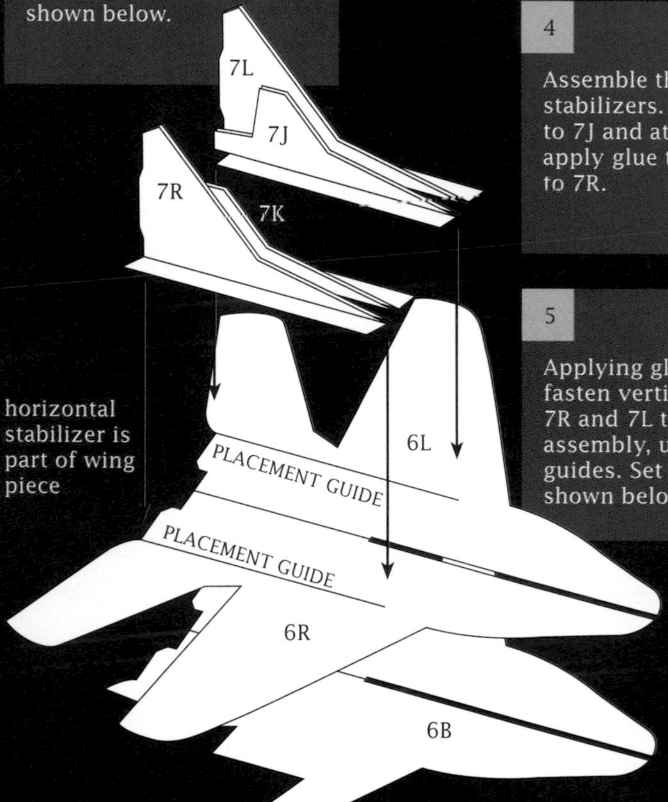

2

Glue pieces 1R and 1L through 5R and 5L to build up fuselage layers, carefully aligning parts.

7L
7J
7R
7K

horizontal stabilizer is part of wing piece

PLACEMENT GUIDE
PLACEMENT GUIDE

6L

5

Applying glue to tabs, fasten vertical stabilizers 7R and 7L to the wing assembly, using placement guides. Set dihedral as shown below.

7

Camber the wings by curving the paper gently between thumb and forefinger. See below.

6R

6B

6

Applying glue to the wing tabs, fasten wing assembly to the fuselage, aligning center lines.

WINGS 2°
VERT STAB 2°

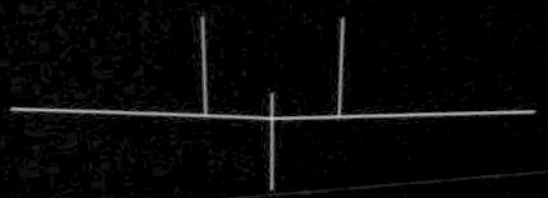

point of maximum camber, 25-30% from front

CORRECT CAMBER

NOTE
• Cut on lines shown in black.
• Score lines in red.
• Use the blue lines as guides for adding details to the plane.
❯ Indicates the front edge of the piece.

PARTS LAYOUT – Fulcrum

The military uses of aircraft pose some unique problems. One is pilot safety. There have been two solutions. One is to make planes pilotless, small, and expendable. The German Buzzbomb was an early example. Such craft can be launched from large bombers while airborne, ramjets (see p 74) giving them a range of great distances at supersonic speed. Computer controlled guidance systems make them fly accurately. They are cruise missiles.

The second solution is to make planes invisible. Ever since the invention of radar in the Second World War, planes are detected long before they are visible to the naked eye, making them easy targets. In response engineers began to design aircraft that were difficult to detect by electronic devices using what is known as *stealth* technology.

Several things make airplanes detectable by electronic devices. One is their overall shape. In order to be stealthy there can be no right-angled surfaces and no protrusions on the airplane. Because jets are already streamlined, they are ideally suited to being made stealthy. The materials used in their construction also affects an airplane's stealthiness. To be stealthy less metal must be used. Another is that most fighters have so many different stores attached beneath their wings and fuselages. To be stealthy these need to be placed inside the fuselage. Yet another is the heat streaming from their jet nozzles. To be

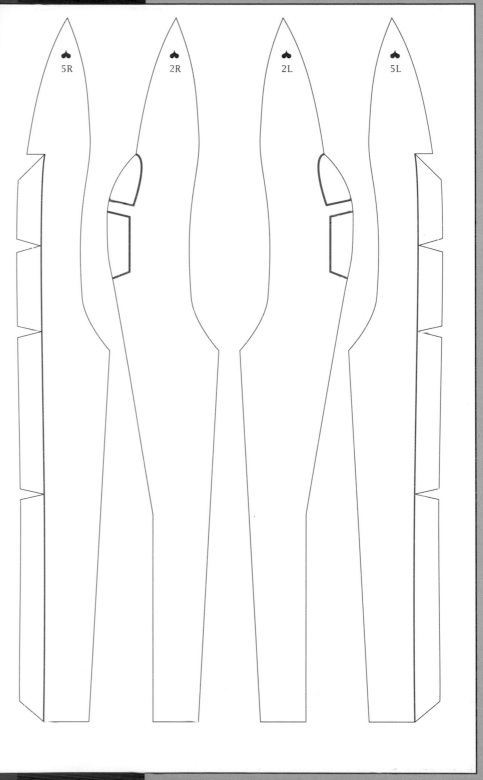

PARTS LAYOUT – Fulcrum

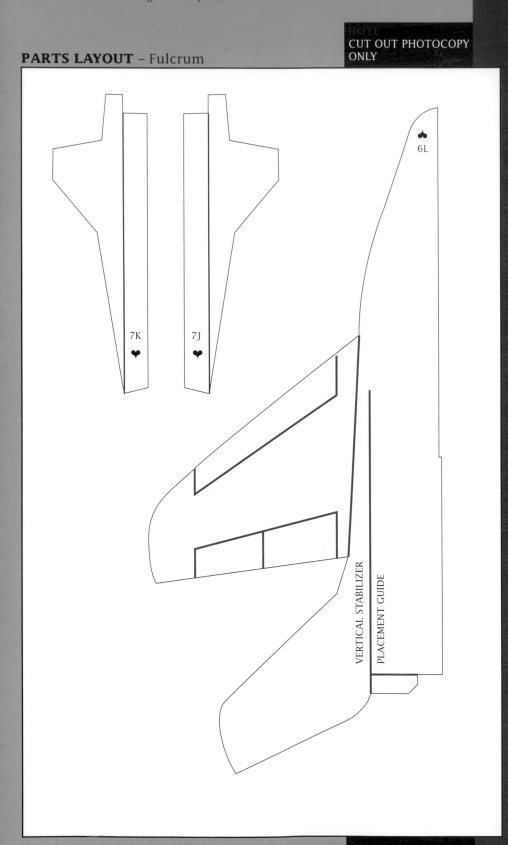

7K ❤

7J ❤

6L ♣

VERTICAL STABILIZER

PLACEMENT GUIDE

stealthy the nozzles need to be shielded.

One of the first stealthy airplanes, however, is anything but smooth. From the Skunkworks at Lockheed came the unique F-117 Nighthawk, designed for nighttime attack operations. **(#13, p 71.)** For this role it need not be fast or maneuverable. This subsonic plane's unusual delta shape, with multi-faceted geometric panels and black skin, make it almost invisible to both electronic devices and, at night, to the naked eye. Although built in 1977, the Nighthawk was kept a secret until it saw extensive use in the Gulf War in 1991.

All future fighters will be stealthy. The Lockheed F-22 Raptor is an example. **(#14, p 77.)** Currently in the development stage, it will come into operation sometime early in the 21st century as a maneuverable, supersonic and supercruise, multi-role fighter, that will replace many current models. It is smooth skinned with no right angles and no protrusions. It is the first fighter design since the Arrow where all stores are carried internally. The Raptor's thrust vectoring jet nozzles are buried and shielded.

private jets

PARTS LAYOUT – Fulcrum

With the increase in size and complexity of businesses, and the placement of outlying facilities in remote locations not serviced by regular jet flights, there was a need for fast transportation for a few people to these areas on a frequent basis. Airplanes, owned and operated by the corporations themselves, were the answer. Many airplane manufacturers build jets to meet this need. The first, the Gates Learjet, in 1963, has been built in large numbers. **(#15, p 83.)** This six-passenger aircraft flies at a speed of about 500 miles per hour and is powered by two turbojet engines. Because of its speed and suitable size, the Learjet also serves as air ambulance in some countries.

Even smaller and simpler jet propelled planes are being built as smaller and smaller turbojet engines are being developed. Some are made as sport planes for private use, others as small business jets. One currently being test flown is the four-seat British CMC Leopard. **(#16, p 89.)** It is the size of the average family car. This 400-mile-per-hour plane is powered by two small turbojet engines.

Increasingly, propellers are being attached to turbojet engines to make turboprops. See p 80. This idea is not new. The Vickers Viscount was the first to do so in 1948. Today, a variety of airplanes are turbo-

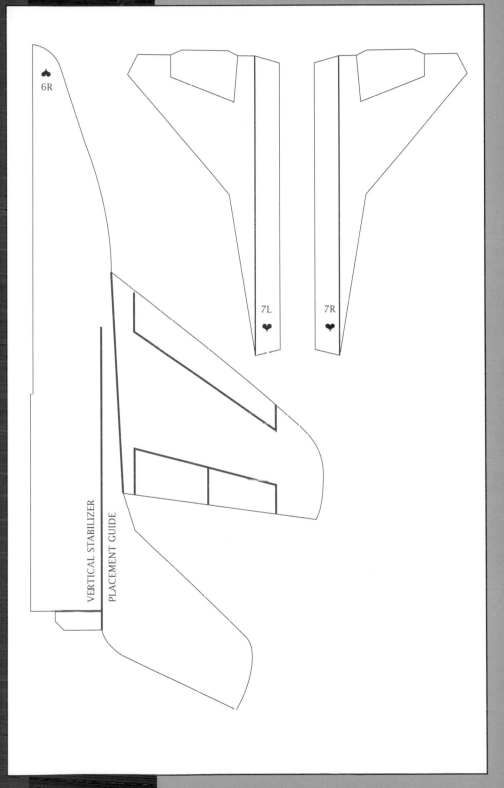

NOTE
• Cut on lines shown in black.
• Score lines in red.
• Use the blue lines as guides for adding details to the plane.
➤ Indicates the front edge of the piece.

PARTS LAYOUT – Fulcrum

prop powered, from crop dusters to airliners. Because these propulsion systems are fuel efficient and extraordinarily quiet, there is increasing use of them for commuter planes on short-trip passenger flights over populated areas.

The future of jet propulsion is bright. It will continue to develop with lighter, more powerful, more fuel-efficient, and quieter propulsion systems in airframes designed for a wide variety of tasks.

Lockheed F-117 Nighthawk
stealth

13

1

Photocopy the parts layouts for this model. Then cut out and prepare the pieces. (See the general instructions beginning on p 4.)

6L
5L
4L
3L
2L
1F
2R
3R
4R
5R
6R

use edges as positioning guides

TAIL

7L

TAIL

7R

7B

2

Glue pieces 1F through 6R and 6L to build up fuselage layers, carefully aligning parts.

7

Camber the wings by curving the paper gently between thumb and forefinger. See below.

3

Bring wing parts 7L and 7R together. Glue piece 7B to the bottom, aligning centers. The V-tail is part of wing piece. Set dihedral of both as shown below.

6

Applying glue to the wing tabs, fasten wing assembly to the fuselage, aligning center lines.

WINGS 5°
V-TAIL 65°

point of maximum camber, 10-20% from front

CORRECT CAMBER

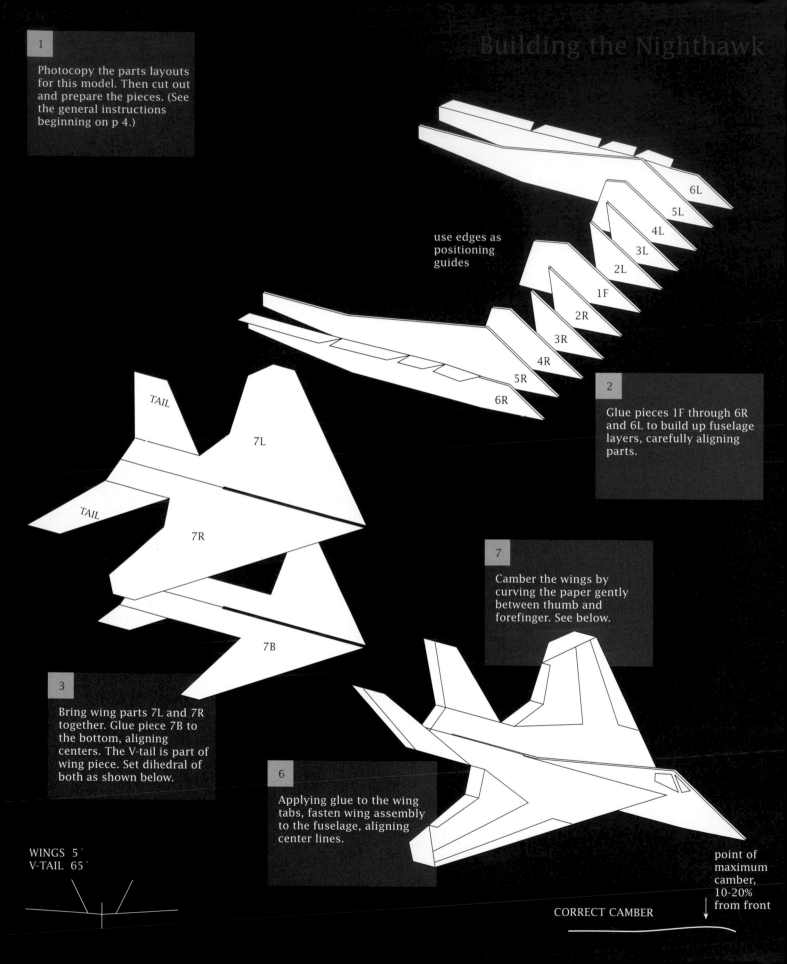

jet propulsion systems

1 THE SIMPLEST JET

The simplest of all jets is the solid-fuel rocket. It has no moving parts and there is no way to control how fast the fuel burns in such an engine or to turn it off once lit. It is either off or on. All the propelling charge is stored right in the engine's combustion chamber, burning from one end to the other until it is all consumed. It burns without air, the oxydizer is contained within the fuel. At the rear end is a nozzle through which the jet of hot combustion gas escapes. The action of the burning gas escaping in one direction causes an equal reaction, propelling the rocket in the opposite direction. Fins help to guide the rocket, pointing it in the direction of flight. This was the Chinese "arrow of flying fire" and is the forerunner of all other modern jets.

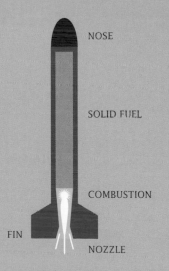

NOSE

SOLID FUEL

COMBUSTION

FIN

NOZZLE

PARTS LAYOUT – Nighthawk

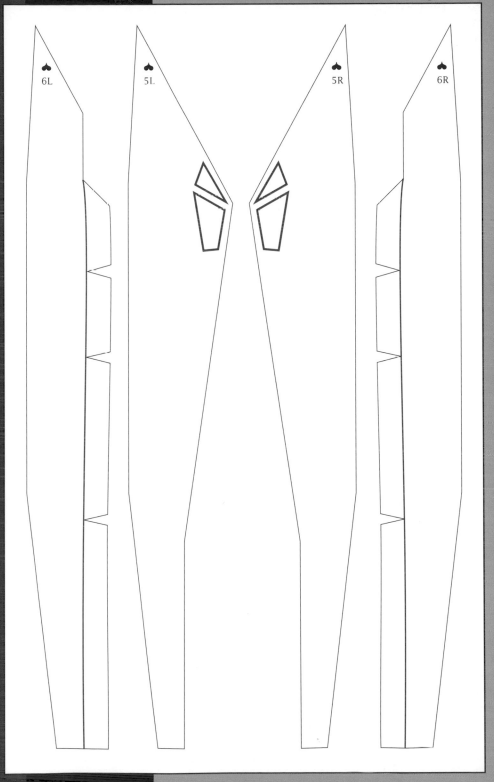

6L   5L   5R   6R

NOTE

- Cut on lines shown in black.
- Score lines in red.
- Use the blue lines as guides for adding details to the plane.
- ❥ Indicates the front edge of the piece.

PARTS LAYOUT – Nighthawk

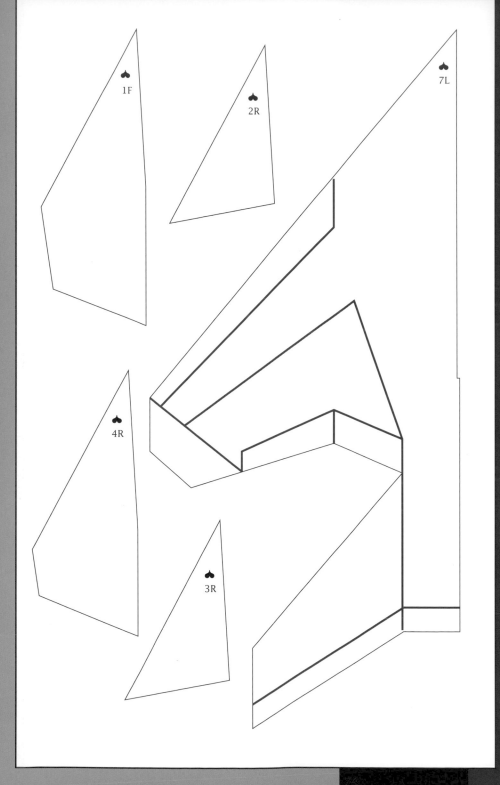

2 RAMJET

As do solid fuel rockets, ramjets have no moving parts. Before a ramjet can operate it must first be set in motion by some other means. A solid fuel rocket is often used. Once the ramjet moves through the air at high speed, air is rammed into the air inlet at the front of the engine. As air enters the engine, it cannot move through the engine fast enough to make room for the new air coming in. The ramming action squeezes the air, compressing it. This makes the air very hot. This hot air then moves back past the fuel inlets, vaporizing the stream of liquid fuel and igniting it. The mixture of fuel and air burns continuously in the combustion chamber. The pressure generated by the combustion sends a flaming exhaust out the jet nozzle. Reaction to this force drives the jet forward. Ramjets operate best at high steady speeds.

AIR INLET

FUEL INLETS

COMBUSTION

JET NOZZLE

NOTE
• Cut on lines shown in black.
• Score lines in red.
• Use the blue lines as guides for adding details to the plane.
❯ Indicates the front edge of the piece.

PARTS LAYOUT – Nighthawk

3 PULSEJET

The pulsejet consists of a tube containing air inlet valves, a combustion chamber having fuel inlets and a spark plug, and an exhaust nozzle. The engine is started by first spraying liquid fuel into the combustion chamber through the fuel inlets while pumping air into the air inlet valves. A spark plug ignites the first charge of fuel/air mixture. The pressure in the combustion chamber rises from the burning and the air valves are forced shut. The hot gases can then escape only out the exhaust nozzle. When all the gas has escaped the pressure drops, opening the air valves. By this time the engine is in motion and fresh air rushes into the vacated combustion chamber. As more fuel is sprayed the still-hot combustion chamber vaporizes the fuel and ignites the fuel/air mixture, repeating the cycle. The combustion cycle repeats over and over many times each second, making pulsejets rather inefficient (and loud).

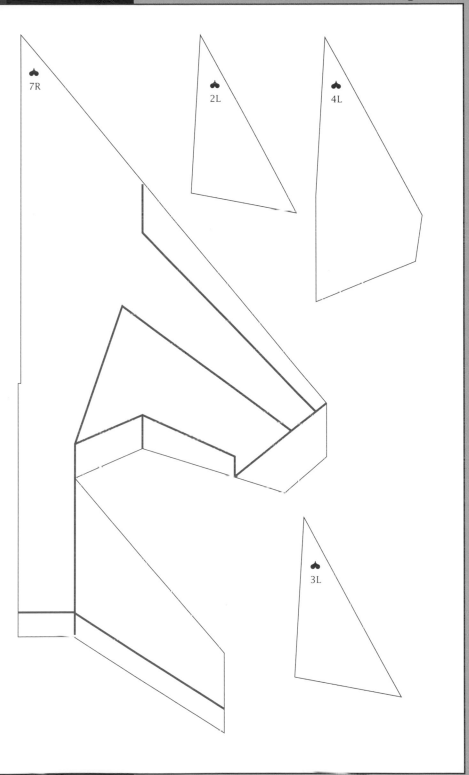

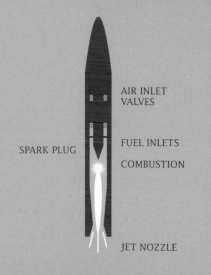

AIR INLET
VALVES

SPARK PLUG

FUEL INLETS

COMBUSTION

JET NOZZLE

PARTS LAYOUT – Nighthawk

♣
7B

4 TURBOJET

This jet engine has an air compressor that consists of a series of discs with fanlike blades around their circumferences. As the discs spin, air is forced by the blades from one set of blades to the next. By the time air has passed through all the blades its pressure has been greatly increased, and in the process has become very hot. This hot compressed air rushes into the combustion chamber where it is mixed with fuel, which vaporizes and ignites from the heat. The heat of combustion greatly expands the volume of the air, which escapes through another disc with blades, called a turbine, located at the back of the combustion chamber. This sets the turbine spinning. The turbine is connected by a shaft to the compressor and keeps it spinning, forcing a steady stream of high pressure hot air into the engine. An afterburner gives a turbojet extra power by spraying additional fuel into the jet nozzle behind the turbine.

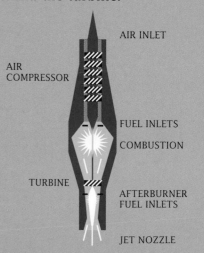

AIR INLET

AIR
COMPRESSOR

FUEL INLETS

COMBUSTION

TURBINE

AFTERBURNER
FUEL INLETS

JET NOZZLE

Lockheed F-22 Raptor
into the 21st century

1

Photocopy the parts layouts for this model. Then cut out and prepare the pieces. (See the general instructions beginning on p 4.)

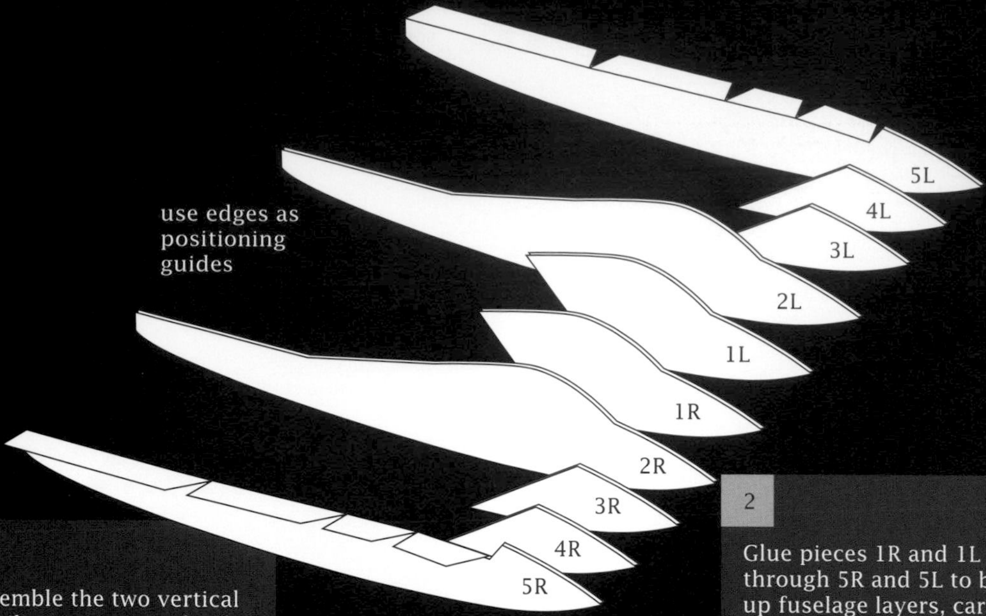

use edges as positioning guides

5L
4L
3L
2L
1L
1R
2R
3R
4R
5R

3

Bring wing parts 6L and 6R together. Glue piece 6B to the bottom, aligning centers. Set dihedral as shown below.

2

Glue pieces 1R and 1L through 5R and 5L to build up fuselage layers, carefully aligning parts.

horizontal stabilizer is part of wing piece

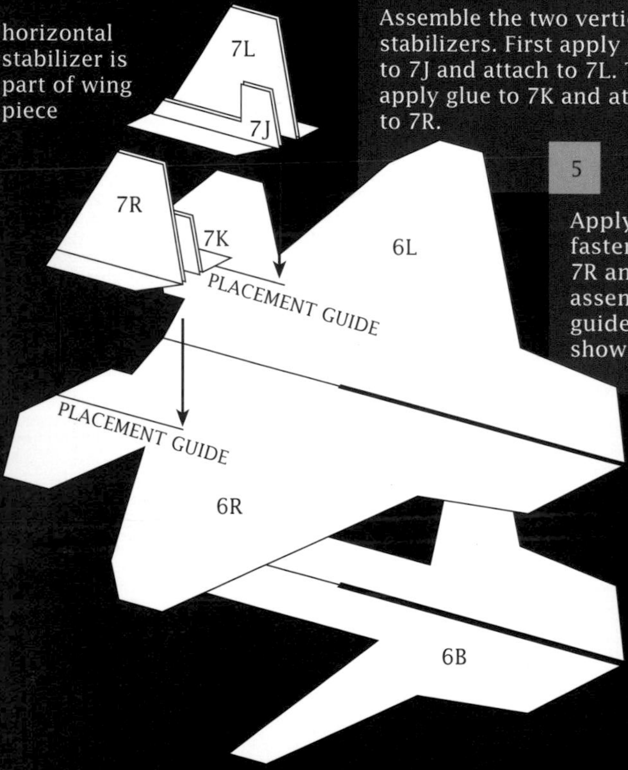

7L
7J

4

Assemble the two vertical stabilizers. First apply glue to 7J and attach to 7L. Then apply glue to 7K and attach to 7R.

7R
7K
PLACEMENT GUIDE
6L

PLACEMENT GUIDE

5

Applying glue to tabs, fasten vertical stabilizers 7R and 7L to the wing assembly, using placement guides. Set dihedral as shown below.

7

Camber the wings by curving the paper gently between thumb and forefinger. See below.

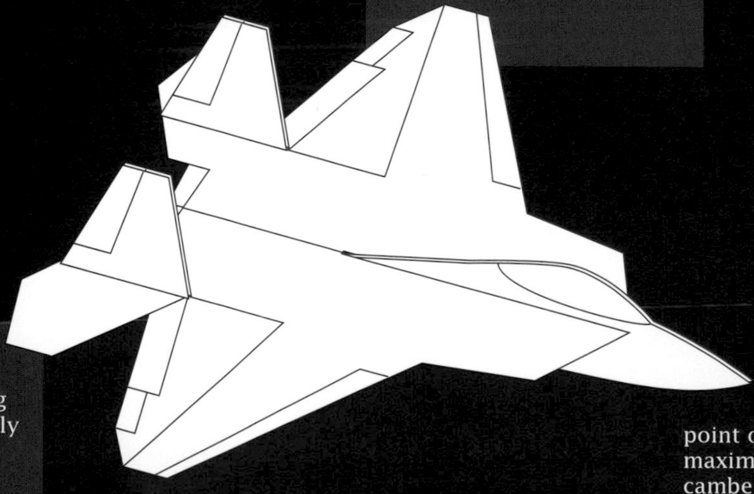

6R

6B

6

Applying glue to the wing tabs, fasten wing assembly to the fuselage, aligning center lines.

WINGS 2°
VERT STAB 2°

point of maximum camber, 10-20% from front

CORRECT CAMBER

NOTE
- Cut on lines shown in black.
- Score lines in red.
- Use the blue lines as guides for adding details to the plane.
- ➤ Indicates the front edge of the piece.

5 FANJET

The propelling power of this engine comes from two sources. The inside core is similar to a turbojet. It has a compressor, combustion chamber with fuel inlets, turbine, and jet nozzle, and is the first source of power. It is different in that it has a second turbine which is connected by a shaft to a large fan ahead of the air compressor. This fan pushes air back into the engine, but only a portion of it enters the compressor. The rest passes around the turbojet core. The fan operates the same as an ordinary propeller, increasing pressure behind it without generating heat, and is the second source of propelling power. These jets have afterburners only when used in fighters. At slow speed fanjets suck much greater amounts of air into the engine. Airplanes using fanjets accelerate and climb faster. Fanjets consume less fuel and are altogether more efficient than turbojets. They are also much quieter, except when afterburners are used.

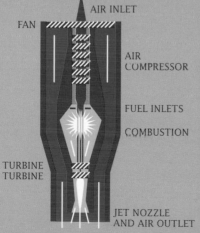

AIR INLET
FAN
AIR COMPRESSOR
FUEL INLETS
COMBUSTION
TURBINE
TURBINE
JET NOZZLE AND AIR OUTLET

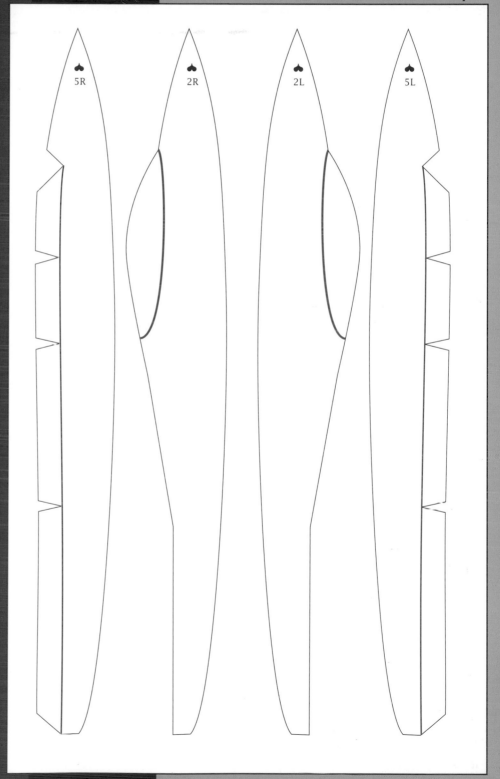

5R   2R   2L   5L

NOTE
• Cut on lines shown in black.
• Score lines in red.
• Use the blue lines as guides for adding details to the plane.
❧ Indicates the front edge of the piece.

PARTS LAYOUT – Raptor

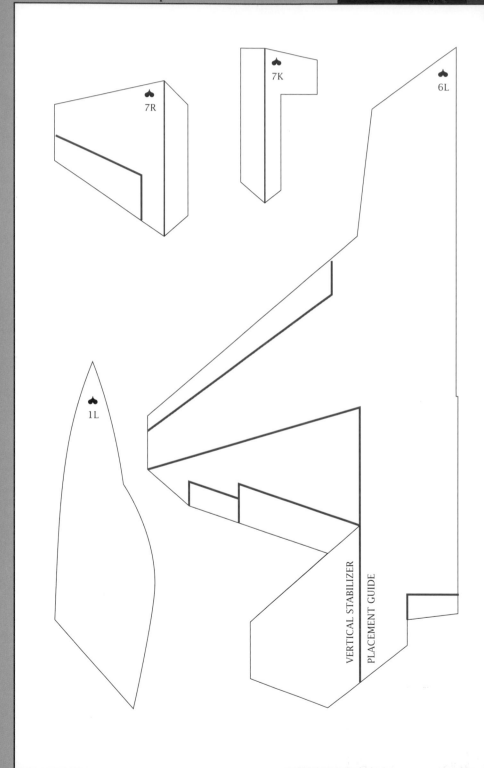

♣ 7R

♣ 7K

♣ 6L

♣ 1L

VERTICAL STABILIZER PLACEMENT GUIDE

6 TURBOPROP

The turboprop consists of a turbojet engine and a regular propeller. As with the fanjet, propelling power comes from two sources, the jet and the propeller, but more power is obtained from the propeller than the jet. As does the fanjet, the turbo-prop has two turbines, one connected to the propeller by a driveshaft and gearbox, the other driving the compressor. The turboprop is most efficient at relatively low speeds, slower than other jets. It is also much quieter than either a piston-driven propeller engine or any other jet.

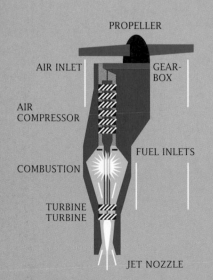

PROPELLER

AIR INLET

GEAR-BOX

AIR COMPRESSOR

FUEL INLETS

COMBUSTION

TURBINE
TURBINE

JET NOZZLE

NOTE
• Cut on lines shown in black.
• Score lines in red.
• Use the blue lines as guides for adding details to the plane.
➤ Indicates the front edge of the piece.

NOTE
CUT OUT PHOTOCOPY
ONLY

7 THRUST VECTORED JET

In most jet engines the internal parts are aligned so that air moves through the engine in a straight line. The jet nozzle is fixed and the thrust is straight out the back. In the future more jet engines will have nozzles made to swivel on hinges, directing the thrust in different directions no longer in line with the engine. This is called vectored thrust. Sideways, upward, and downward thrust in an airplane increases its maneuverability. Additionally, secondary hinged nozzles give added maneuverability. They can be of different sizes and be located remotely, connected by ducts to the engine. Small nozzles are called puffer jets. They are esssential for hovering flight.

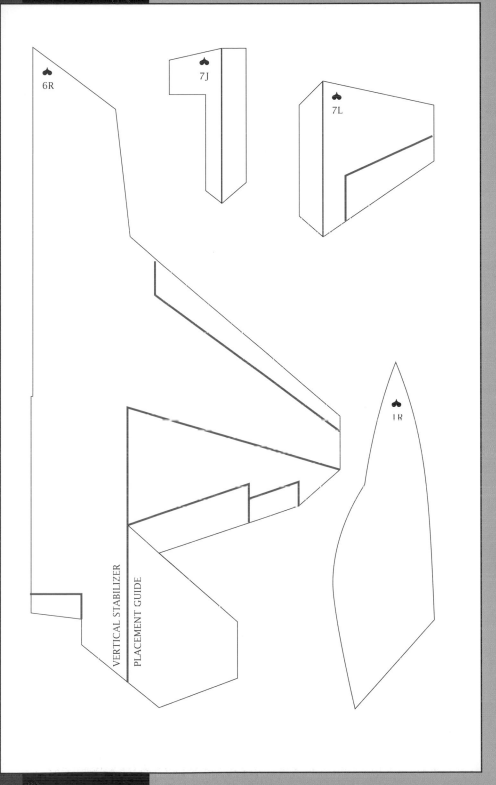

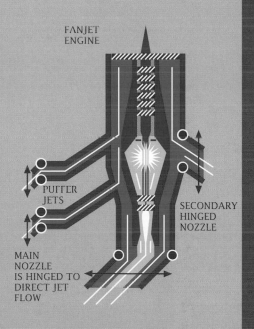

FANJET
ENGINE

PUFFER
JETS

SECONDARY
HINGED
NOZZLE

MAIN
NOZZLE
IS HINGED TO
DIRECT JET
FLOW

VERTICAL STABILIZER
PLACEMENT GUIDE

6R

7J

7L

1R

PARTS LAYOUT – Raptor

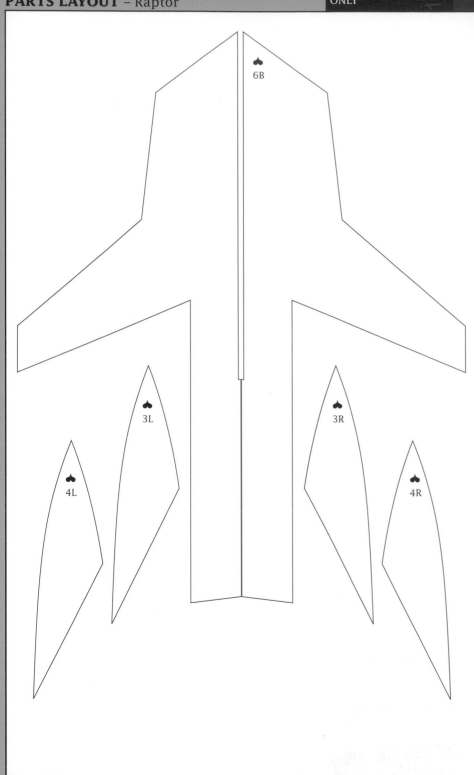

flying the paper planes

The paper jets are gliders. A paper glider's loss of height as gravity pulls it downward and forward is called sink. Every paper glider has a particular *rate of sink*. The amount of sink in relation to a glider's forward movement, is known as the *glide ratio*. At a constant airspeed the ratio of the lifting force of the wings and the resistant force of drag is exactly equal to the glide ratio. Therefore for a paper glider to have a high glide ratio, drag must be kept at a minimum. It must have efficient wings and be made without rough edges.

Proper elevator adjustment is important to maximize performance in the flight of any airplane, including paper ones. (See p 36.) In aircraft of conventional configuration the horizontal stabilizer and the elevator provide a counterbalancing force compensating for the automatic downward pitching motion due to the center of gravity's location ahead of the center of lift. Furthermore, in all gliding flight, controlling pitch is especially important because it also controls airspeed. Airspeed, in turn, affects the glide ratio and overall performance of the plane. Every paper airplane has an optimum speed for a best glide ratio. This is its cruising speed. Adjusting a plane to fly at this speed is called *trimming for cruise.*

Gates Learjet
business jet

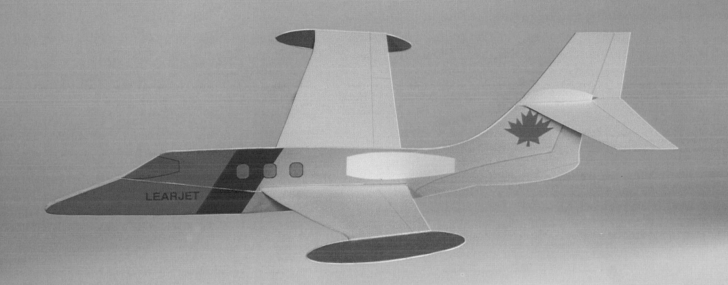

15

1

Photocopy the parts layouts for this model. Then cut out and prepare the pieces. (See the general instructions beginning on p 4.)

use wing opening slits and edges as positioning guides

7L
6L
5L
4L
3L
2L
1F
2R
3R
4R
5R
6R
7R

2

Glue pieces 1F through 7R and 7L to build up fuselage layers, carefully aligning parts.

3

Glue piece 8B to the bottom of wing part 8W, aligning centers. Set dihedral as shown below.

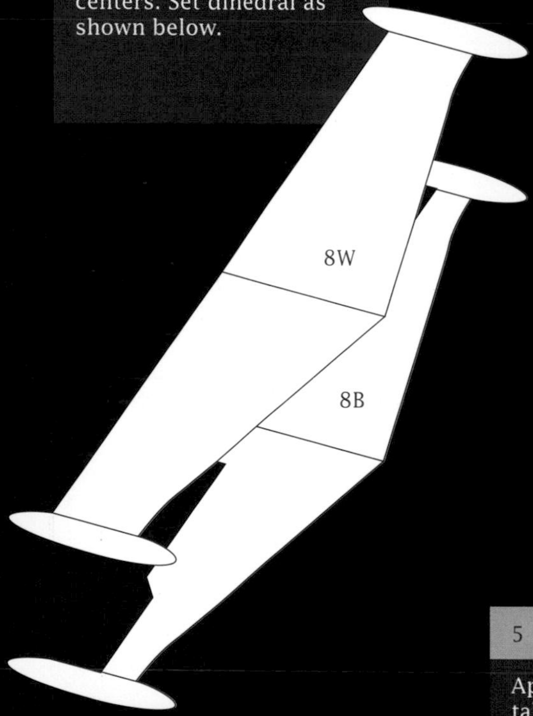

4

Applying glue to the tail tabs, fasten horizontal stabilizer 9S to the fuselage.

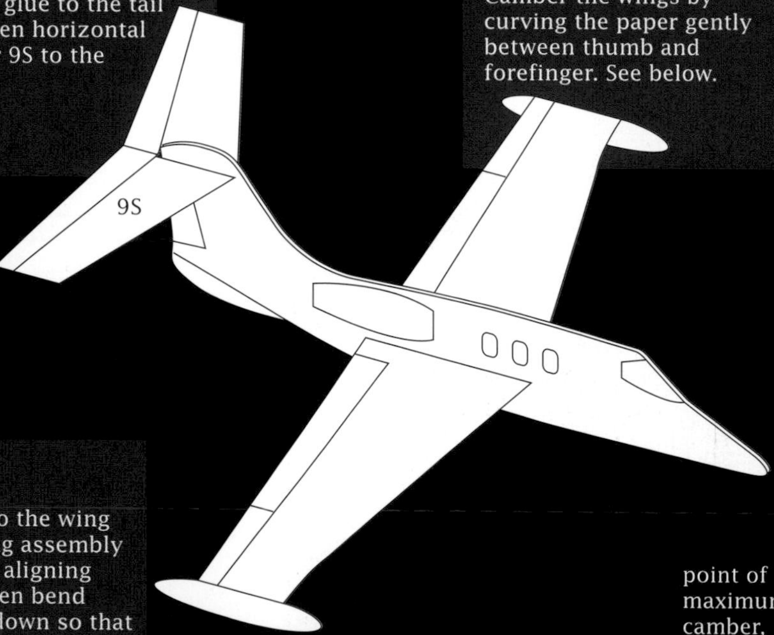

6

Camber the wings by curving the paper gently between thumb and forefinger. See below.

8W

8B

9S

5

Applying glue to the wing tabs, fasten wing assembly to the fuselage, aligning center lines. Then bend wing tip tanks down so that they are vertical.

WINGS 15°
HOR STAB 0°

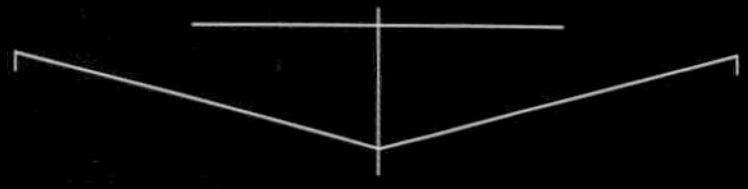

point of maximum camber, 25-30% from front

CORRECT CAMBER

NOTE
- Cut on lines shown in black.
- Score lines in red.
- Use the blue lines as guides for adding details to the plane.
- ❯ Indicates the front edge of the piece.

HANDLING PAPER AIRPLANES

Pick up and hold paper airplanes by the nose, their sturdiest part. *Never* lift them by the wings or tail; this will distort their aerodynamic shape.

PREFLIGHT INSPECTION

After a paper plane is finished and the glue completely dried, do a preflight inspection and make any necessary adjustments.

Examine the plane thoroughly from the front, back, top, bottom, and each side. Check for parts that appear bent or twisted. Correct any defects. Gently massage the paper to work out bends and twists. Each side must be *exactly* like the other — shape, size, camber, dihedral — a paper airplane must be symmetrical.

TEST FLIGHTS

The objective of test flights is to trim (adjust) the glider for straight and level flight at *its best speed*.

Hold the fuselage between thumb and forefinger just behind the plane's center of gravity. Throw it *gently* with a straight ahead motion (not as though it were a baseball). A paper plane flies best at only one speed. Throwing it too hard will cause it to climb sharply, stall, and dive to the ground, or do a complete loop. Once you have trimmed the plane for good flight performance, differ-

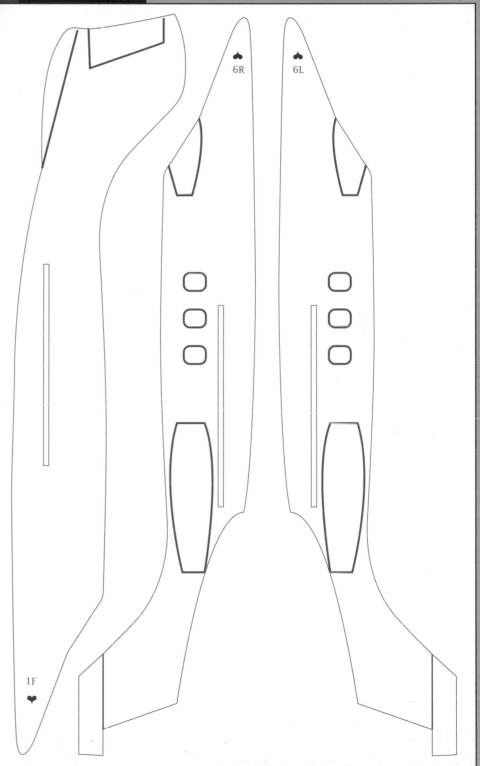

NOTE
CUT OUT PHOTOCOPY ONLY

PARTS LAYOUT – Learjet

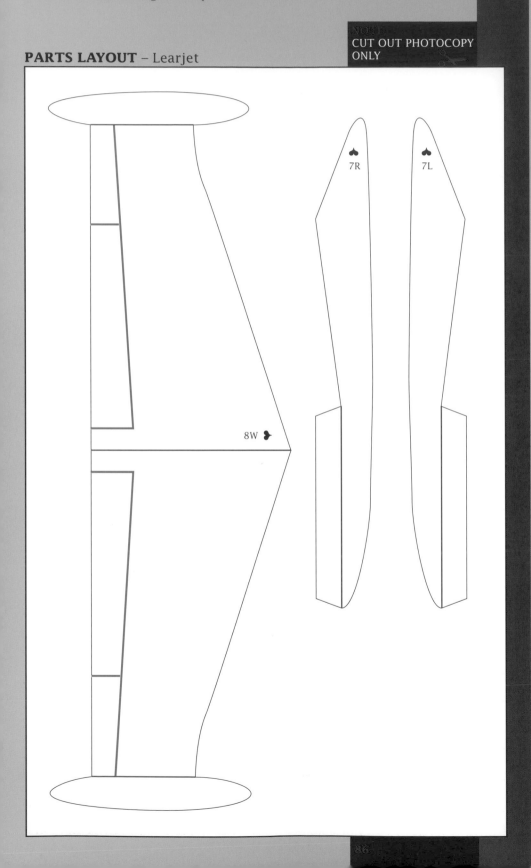

ent throwing techniques can be tried. Try to test fly in calm conditions so that each flight is more predictable.

Sometimes, on the very first flight, a paper plane is unbalanced in every way at the same time. Therefore it is necessary to separate the control functions in one's mind and deal with them one at a time.

To correct a dive the elevator needs adjusting by bending it up slightly to give positive trim. Continue making test flights concentrating on this one adjustment until this control input is correct. In normal gliding flight there should be slight positive elevator trim.

If a paper plane banks and turns in either direction it is always due to one wing producing more lift than the other. First make sure that the camber is *identical* in both wings along their entire lengths. If camber is slightly greater in one wing, that wing will produce more lift, causing it to rise — the plane will bank and turn in the opposite direction. Second, make sure that the wings are not twisted. The wingtip that is lower at the trailing edge (thereby having a greater angle of attack) will cause that wing to produce more lift, and it will rise — the plane will bank and turn in the opposite direction. Untwist the wings to correct this problem. Continue mak-

NOTE
- Cut on lines shown in black.
- Score lines in red.
- Use the blue lines as guides for adding details to the plane.
- ➤ Indicates the front edge of the piece.

ing test flights concentrating on this adjustment until the wings are correct.

A slightly bent fuselage will also cause the plane to turn by yawing left or right. Make the fuselage as straight as possible. For a final correction adjust the rudder by bending it in the opposite direction to the turn.

If the plane climbs, loses speed, and pitches down sharply (stalls), the elevator needs to be bent down slightly. However, if this problem cannot be corrected without the elevator being bent down below the straight level, the airplane's center of gravity is too far back and additional ballast is needed in the nose. Glue additional layers of paper into the nose. Again, continue making test flights until this problem is corrected.

Continue to make test flights until the plane flies straight and level in a gentle glide.

EXTENDING THE FLIGHT

If a paper airplane is launched into the wind the increased relative airspeed would make the lightweight plane climb very steeply, and perhaps stall, and dive to the ground, or, if the elevator is bent up slightly, do a complete loop. When launched with the wind, wind speed is added to actual airspeed, increasing the ability to cover distance over the ground. But in a downwind launch the plane may stall if the wind is too

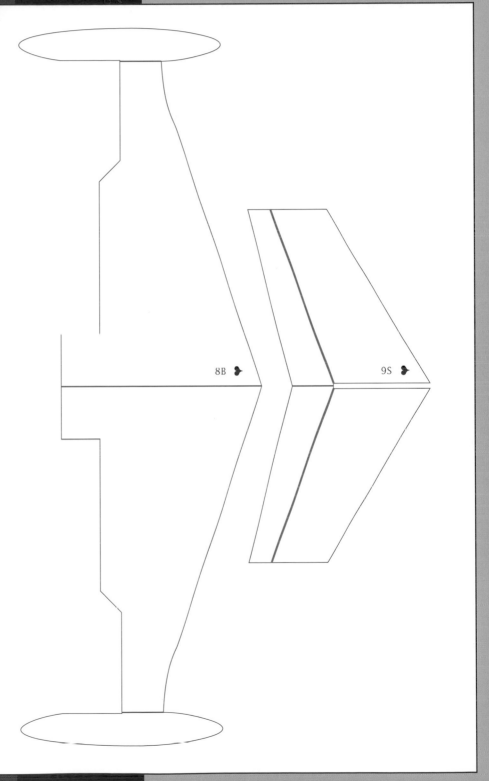

8B ➤

9S ➤

NOTE
• Cut on lines shown in black.
• Score lines in red.
• Use the blue lines as guides for adding details to the plane.
❧ Indicates the front edge of the piece.

PARTS LAYOUT – Learjet

NOTE
CUT OUT PHOTOCOPY
ONLY

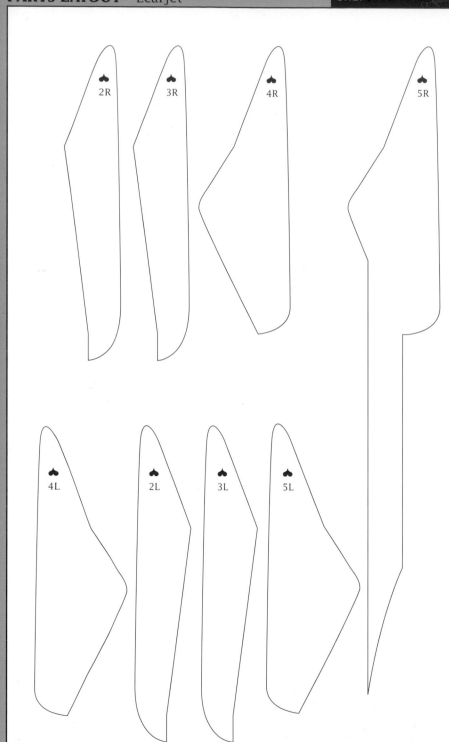

strong because of the decreased relative airspeed. To avoid these tendencies, launch the plane *across the wind*, letting it turn downwind gradually.

Another way to fly a paper plane is to begin the flight with a high launch. The plane should be trimmed for a gentle left or right turn. (If the pilot is right-handed, trim for a gentle turn to the left.) For making a left turn adjust the control surfaces. Make these trim adjustments in very slight increments until the desired turn rate is achieved.

Launch the plane in an inclined position with considerable force upward and away from your body (about 45 degrees), across the wind. It gains altitude from the force of the throw, but loses speed as it climbs. The dihedral causes the wings to level out. Once level, the left-handed trim banks the glider into a gentle turn downwind at the top of its climb. Because of the altitude gained by the high launch, the descent should be a good long glide.

Because paper is a relatively unstable material it may be necessary to readjust the planes after every few flights. Gusty wind conditions can make it impossible to fly such lightweight planes successfully.

CMC Leopard
personal jet

16

1

Photocopy the parts layouts for this model. Then cut out and prepare the pieces. (See the general instructions beginning on p 4.)

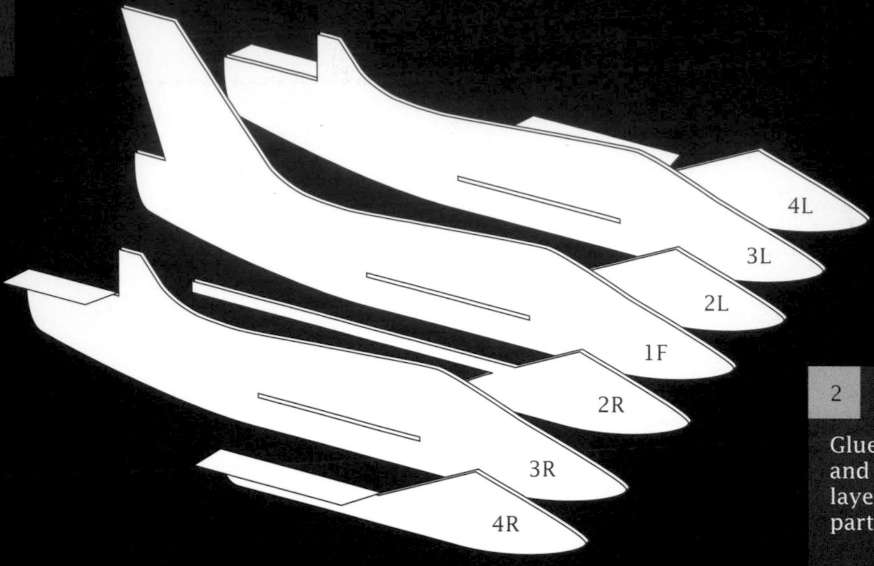

4L

3L

2L

1F

2R

3R

4R

use wing opening slits and edges as positioning guides

2

Glue pieces 1F through 4R and 4L to build up fuselage layers, carefully aligning parts.

3

Glue piece 5B to the bottom of wing part 5W, aligning centers. Set dihedral as shown below.

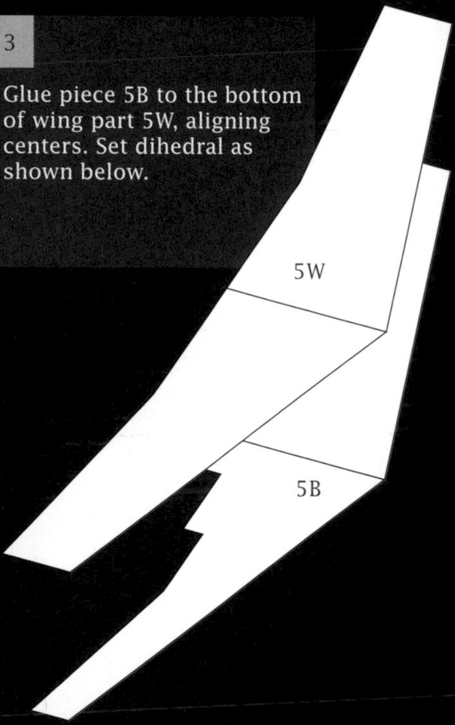

5W

5B

4

Applying glue to the tail tabs, fasten horizontal stabilizer 6S to the fuselage.

6

Camber the wings by curving the paper gently between thumb and forefinger. See below.

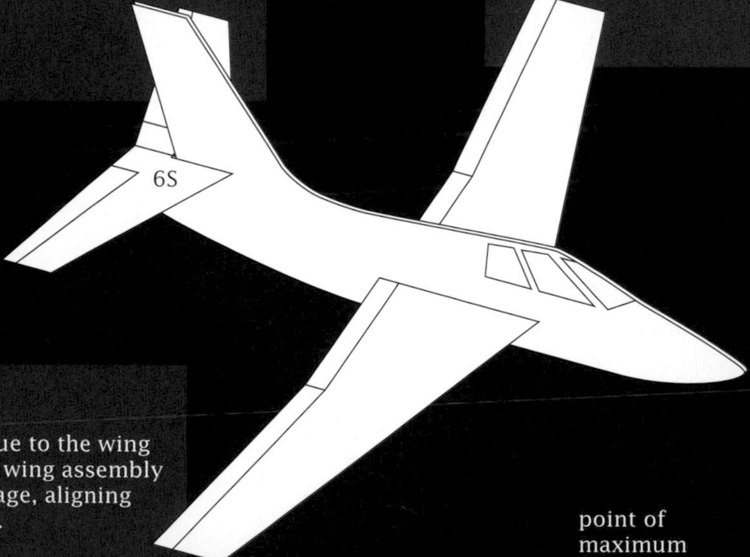

6S

5

Applying glue to the wing tabs, fasten wing assembly to the fuselage, aligning center lines.

WINGS 15°
HOR STAB -15°

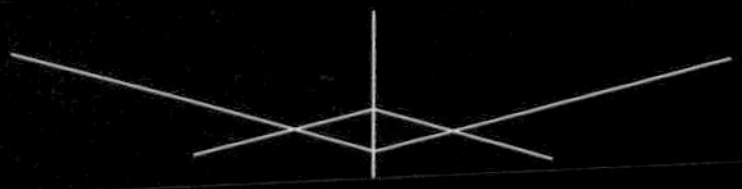

point of maximum camber, 25-30% from front

CORRECT CAMBER

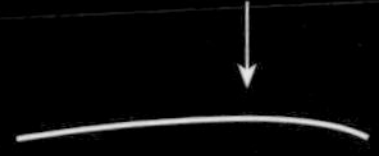

STORING THE PLANES

When carefully handled, these paper planes can last a long time. To keep them from becoming damaged or warped when not in use they need proper storage. One way is to hang them by the nose from a line using clothes pins.

By stringing the line inside a large cardboard box, a handy portable storage "hangar" can be made. (See below.)

FIGURE 12

A portable "hangar" consists of a line with clothes pins inside a cardboard box.

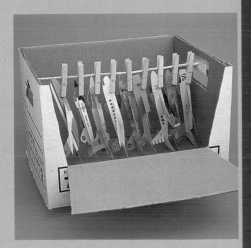

NOTE
• Cut on lines shown in black.
• Score lines in red.
• Use the blue lines as guides for adding details to the plane.
❯ Indicates the front edge of the piece.

NOTE
CUT OUT PHOTOCOPY ONLY

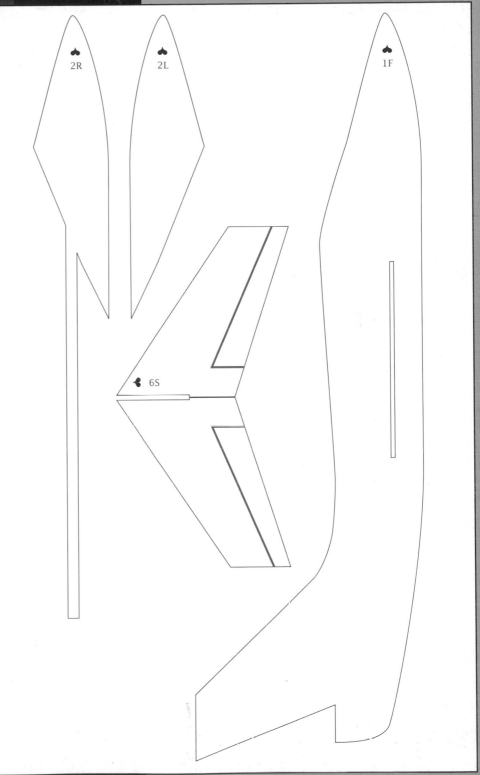

2R

2L

1F

6S

NOTE
• Cut on lines shown in black.
• Score lines in red.
• Use the blue lines as guides for adding details to the plane.
❥ Indicates the front edge of the piece.

PARTS LAYOUT – Leopard

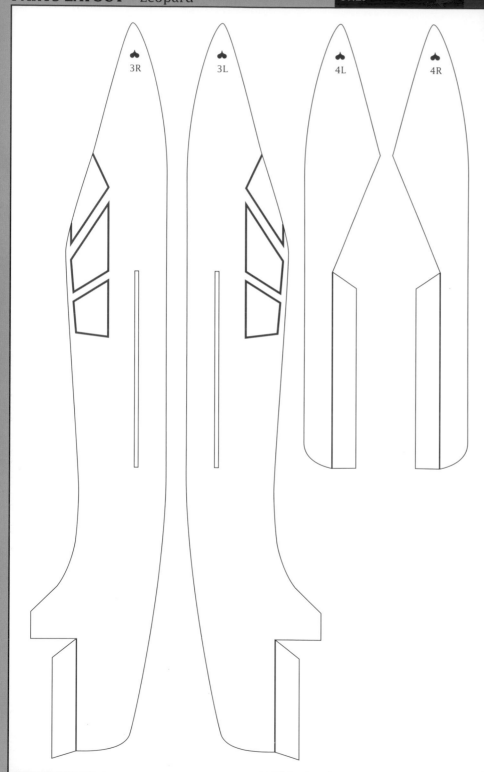

DISPLAYING THE PLANES

The paper jets make fine displays. Display mounts can be made from the same index card stock as the planes, according to the following steps.

a) Cut card into strip 1 in x 8 in (2.5cm x 20 cm).

b) Measure, dividing the strip into 4 equal sections.

FIGURE 13

Making a display mount for the paper jet airplanes.

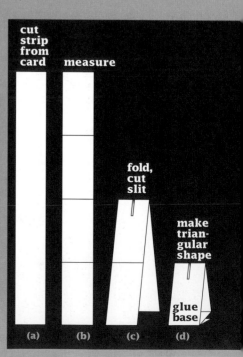

cut strip from card | measure | fold, cut slit | make triangular shape | glue base

(a)   (b)   (c)   (d)

c) Fold strip in half. Cut a slit into the folded-over end.

d) Bend strip to form a triangular shape so that the two outer sections overlap to make a base. Glue the overlapping sections.

e) The plane's fuselage sits in the slit, balancing at its center of gravity. (See below.)

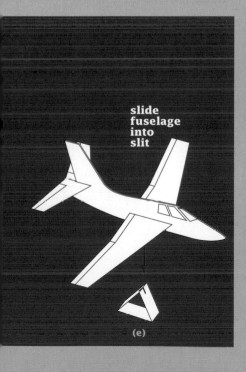

slide
fuselage
into
slit

(e)

PARTS LAYOUT – Leopard

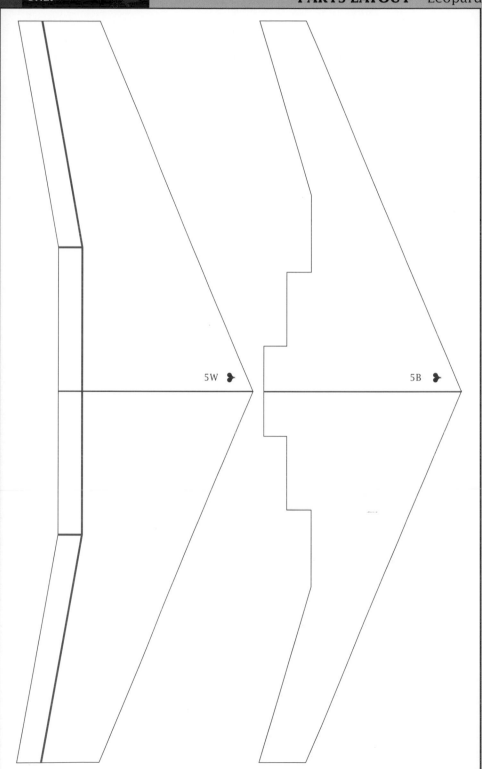

5W ❯

5B ❯

Aeronautical terms

OTHER BOOKS BY NORMAN SCHMIDT

Discover Aerodynamics With Paper Airplanes. Pequis, Winnipeg, 1991.

Best Ever Paper Airplanes. Sterling/Tamos, New York, 1994.

Super Paper Airplanes. Sterling/Tamos, New York, 1996.

Paper Birds That Fly. Sterling/Tamos, New York, 1996.

The Great Kite Book. Sterling/Tamos, New York, 1997.

Fabulous Paper Gliders. Sterling/Tamos, New York, 1998.

Marvellous Mini Kites. Sterling/Tamos, New York, 1998.

FURTHER READING

Boyne, Walter J. *The Leading Edge*. Workman, New York, 1986.

Taylor, Michael J.H. *History of Flight*. Crescent, New York, 1990.

Wood, Derek. *World Aircraft Recognition Handbook* Jane's, Coulsdon, 1992.

Aspect ratio   The length of a wing in relation to its width. A square has an aspect ratio of 1.

Ailerons   Surfaces on the trailing edges of wings that control roll.

Airfoil   A lift generating surface; a wing.

Airframe   Those parts of an airplane (frame and skinned surfaces) that give it the ability to fly.

Angle of attack   The downward slant, from front to back, of a wing to increase lift.

Attitude   The roll, pitch, and yaw of an aircraft in flight, and the direction it is pointing in relation to the horizon.

Banking   Raising the outside wing and lowering the inside wing during a turn.

Camber   The convex curvature of the upper surface of a wing.

Center of gravity   The point on an aircraft where its weight appears to be concentrated.

Center of lift   The point on an aircraft where its lift appears to be concentrated.

Chord   The measurement of a wing from front to back.

Control surfaces   Small flat hinged surfaces on the trailing edges of wings and tail used to maintain equilibrium and maneuver an airplane.

Dihedral angle   The upward slanting of wings away from the fuselage.

Drag   The resistance of air on moving objects.

Elevator   Control surface on the trailing edge of the horizontal stabilizer used to control pitch.

Fly-by-wire   Aircraft control surfaces that operate electronically rather than mechanically.

Fuselage   The body of an airplane.

Gravity   The force of the earth keeping objects on the ground and giving them weight.

Horizontal stabilizer   A flat horizontal surface directs the flow of air in aid of maintaining equilibrium.

Leading edge   The front edge of an aircraft part.

Lift   The force generated by the wings that counteracts the force of gravity.

Maneuver   Skilfully making an airplane move in the correct manner and fly in the desired direction.

Pitch   The rotation of an airplane causing its nose to go up or down.

Roll   The rotation of an airplane causing the wingtips to rise or fall.

Rudder   Control surface on the trailing edge of the vertical stabilizer used to control yaw.

Shockwave   The pileup of sound waves around an object traveling at the speed of sound.

Sonic boom   The explosive sound of the shockwave being generated by an aircraft passing by at supersonic speed.

Sonic speed (sound barrier)   The speed at which sound waves move through the air.

Stall   The condition that occurs when a wing's angle of attack is too great.

Strakes   Small leading edge wing extensions at the wing root for added lift.

Streamlining   Shaping an airframe so that air flowing around it creates the least amount of drag.

Supercruise   An airplane flying at supersonic speed for an extended time.

Supersonic   The speed of an object greater than the speed of sound.

Thermal barrier   The amount of heat generated by drag that an airframe can withstand.

Thrust   The force needed to move an airplane forward.

Trailing edge   The back edge of an aircraft part.

Trim   The adjustment of control surfaces so that an airplane in flight does not roll, pitch, or yaw.

Vertical stabilizer   A flat vertical surface that directs the flow of air in aid of maintaining equilibrium.

Vortex   The air that swirls in a circular manner behind each wingtip as air slips from the high pressure area below to the low pressure area above.

Wing loading   The amount of weight a given area of wing is required to lift.

Wing span   The measurement from wingtip to wingtip.

Yaw   The rotation of an airplane causing its nose to go left or right.

Index